{ 10 Things } I Want My Husband to Know

ANNIE CHAPMAN

HARVEST HOUSE PUBLISHERS

EUGENE, OREGON

Cover photo © photos.com

Cover by Koechel Peterson Associates, Inc., Minneapolis, Minnesota

10 THINGS I WANT MY HUSBAND TO KNOW
Copyright © 2007 by Annie Chapman
Published by Harvest House Publishers
Eugene, Oregon 97402
www.harvesthousepublishers.com

Library of Congress Cataloging-in-Publication Data
Chapman, Annie.
  10 things I want my husband to know / Annie Chapman.
     p. cm.
  ISBN-13: 978-0-7369-1892-3 (pbk.)
  ISBN-10: 0-7369-1892-2
  1. Husbands—Religious life. 2. Husbands—Conduct of life. 3. Marriage—Religious aspects—
Christianity. 4. Husband and wife. 5. Man–woman relationships—Religious aspects—Christianity.
I. Title.
  BV4528.3.C42 2007
  248.8'44—dc22
                                                                    2006022299

Contents

Building a Marriage That Sparkles

MY LIFE AS A MARRIED WOMAN began on March 29, 1975, when I stood in front of family and friends in a quaint, little Methodist church and made some serious promises to a young man sporting an Art Garfunkel-style hairdo. My bushy-haired beloved was wearing lime-green polyester slacks, cowboy boots, and a homemade muslin shirt. He looked soooooooo "far out." Since Steve and I were products of the hippie era of the late 1960s and early 70s, we decided it would not be cool to repeat vows that had been recited for eons. No, in our youthful exuberance for being different and with love oozing out of every pore of our enlightened bodies, we were convinced that we knew more than those who had come before us. Hence, we decided to create our own vows.

When it came time for the covenants to be exchanged during the marriage ceremony, Steve frantically realized he'd left our carefully crafted words of commitment in his Bible that was sitting on a windowsill far across the sanctuary. Alrighty then! With no help from our cheat-sheets, we were on our own to come up with something memorable and meaningful to say to one another.

I have no idea what lofty, sincerely optimistic promises we made to one another that day. And, sadly, we will never know what was spoken. The 8-track tape recorder (yes, you read it right...an 8-track!) that was supposed to record our ceremony was unfortunately placed beside a young, brain-dead couple who decided to bring their newborn infant to our wedding. When we eagerly rewound the tape to listen to our heartwarming words of commitment, all we heard was the screeching wails of a baby who was not enjoying our wedding. Even though our pledges of love and devotion were not documented on tape that rainy day, I can assure you we meant every word we said. Now, these many decades later, we are still bound by those love-struck promises...whatever they were.

I must admit that being married to my husband, Steve, these many years has been, by far, the easiest job—and joy—I've ever had. My experience has thankfully been nothing like one spouse who was asked, "How long have you been married?" The reply was, "It's been five years of marital bliss-ters!" Much to the contrary, my years are best described by the old song from my far-distant days of youth called "To Know Him Is to Love Him."

One of the things about Steve I cherish most is that he tries to live by the biblical directive to husbands found in 1 Peter 3:7: "Husbands...live with your wives in an understanding way." I know it might sound too good to be true, but Steve really does want to know how I feel and even urges me to tell him. For example, I remember distinctly a specific moment in our dating days that told me he cared about what I thought. It happened when Steve wanted to take me to dinner. When I sat down in the passenger seat of the 1950 Chevy he was driving, he asked, "Where would you like to go eat?"

I answered, "Wherever you want to eat."

He asked again, "Where would *you* like to eat?"

Again I said in a pseudo-submissive tone, "Wherever you'd like to eat."

His response was direct but delivered with gentleness. "If I didn't want to know where you'd like to eat, I wouldn't ask." That was the day I realized it was safe and even appropriate to express my desires and needs. How grateful I am for that revelation as well as the freedom. Others have not been as fortunate.

For some women, sharing their deepest concerns as wives, as well as their sincere wishes about how their husbands handle their roles in the relationship, is the greatest challenge they've ever faced. And then there are the wives who are in marriages that fall between these two positions. Their marriages are good but they wonder if they can be even better. *Ten Things I Want My Husband to Know* will help you build a stronger, more dynamic union.

In my research, that included conversations with wives regarding what they wanted their husbands to know, the following issues rose to the top. A wife longs for her husband to understand that:

- she really *wants* to love him and feel loved in return
- she wants to fully embrace and achieve the God-ordained, scripturally ordered cooperation in the home
- she wants to truly enjoy the privilege of sexual intimacy without guilt or regret
- she wants to bridge the divide that occurs as a result of the everyday challenges of juggling finances, children, hobbies, and in-laws
- she wants the comfort of knowing that both of them will bravely face the sometimes daunting issues of health and aging
- a deep and abiding respect for one another is the foundation for their strong and lasting relationship

The good news is that while it may be a very real challenge for a wife to help her husband see and feel how emotionally important these issues are to her, it is not only possible to do so, but it can be done with expectations of great results. To live these principles and communicate them to your husband takes some good, solid insights along with a little feminine finesse. The finesse is something you already possess. What I am offering in this book are the insights and the nuts and bolts of putting them into practice.

Within these pages is a collection of wisdom gleaned from various resources. First and foremost, the very best insight I can pass along to you comes from the life-changing Word of God. Nothing else on earth is capable of doing what God's written Word can do. Hebrews 4:12-13 reveals that it can literally cut through the hardest of fleshly armor, that it lays bare our hearts. With our lives open to the Great Physician, He then can repair and prepare our hearts so that they can beat in harmony with those we love.

In addition to scriptural insights, I offer my own experiences as a married woman of more than 30 years, as well as contributions from other written sources. I conducted a nonscientific survey by handing out questionnaires to hundreds of women and some of their husbands. The knowledge they generously shared from their collective decades of marriage is also included in this book. With their unique perspectives and priceless participation, you'll find this book even more helpful and practical.

Though I realize there are more than ten things a wife wants her husband to know, I've focused on the crucial concerns for married women. Whether you have been a spouse for a few days or many years, I am confident you will find this book interesting and helpful in making your marriage deeper and more fulfilling.

May God bless each of you as you read these chapters and talk with your husbands.

1

I Want My Husband to Know

I Will Love Him with Pure, Unconditional Love

WHEN ANY OF MY SINGLE, but soon-to-be-married friends would get together and drool over bride magazines and giggle with anticipation while they picked out their wedding dresses, I was the one in the group who would be throwing barbs and jeers their way. When one of them would speak in dreamy terms about Mr. Right and how all she wanted was to be a wife and mother, I was quick to offer my skeptical retorts about screaming babies, poopy diapers, and insensitive, demanding husbands. There was no doubt in my mind that I was destined to be a single, independent, career woman who would never let a man tell her what to do.

All of that was true...until after my college years when I rekindled my friendship with Steve Chapman. Although we had gone to the same middle school and high school, our relationship had never progressed past the "Hey, how are you doing?" stage. I will admit that during the last couple of years of high school, I began to quietly take special notice of him. In fact, that growing interest led me to do something totally out of my character and rather a bit conniving. I lured Steve to my parents' house in the country one cold, autumn morning. How did I do that? I enticed him to come to our farm by openly bragging that my brother had bagged an 11-point buck. For you nonhunters that's a really *big* deer. And for Steve, an avid deer hunter, that's a really big deal. Telling a hunter where he can find a big buck is like telling a woman where she can find designer shoes for $10.

Well, the plan worked, sort of. Steve did come to my house. But the only thing on his mind was hunting! (You can read more about this interesting time—and get your husband a great book—in Steve's bestselling *A Look at Life from a Deer Stand.*) Suffice it to say, enough of my little scheme paid off and Steve fell in love. Of course, it was our farm that won his heart, but, hey, you have to start somewhere! The good news is that because I understood that the way to a hunter's heart is through his treestand, we ended up getting married in 1975 and have stayed married these many years.

When Steve and I were first married, my greatest desire was to be a good, loving, supportive wife. Despite all the negative feelings and ugly words I had spouted about marriage, once I committed to the idea I embraced very lofty expectations of what it should be. I was determined to create a loving, happy environment for both me and my husband.

Looking back I realize that perhaps I was a little paranoid about doing the marriage thing right because I had been so judgmental of others in the past. I recall talking to a friend of mine who had gotten married. I was single and skeptical of whether this "love stuff" was really practical. As we were talking, the young bride said, "Did you see us when we drove up to your house? We've been married four whole months, and we're still sitting close to one another when we drive." Her face was beaming with pride at what a good job they were doing at the "marriage game." My reply was anything but encouraging. I said, "That's fine. But let me see how you treat each other after four *years.*"

Wasn't that mean? It was only one of the many doubtful things I said about matrimony. What I didn't realize was that all the negative words I had picked off the vine of my disdain for marriage were the ingredients in the humble juice I was making for myself. In November of 1974 I became a blushing bride-to-be and the time had come for me to swallow those words.

The one and only song I have ever written by myself was penned during Steve's and my engagement. I've always wondered how many other young girls could have written these same lines.

Never Say Never

I told my mama, "Don't worry about me.
I'll never go crazy, I'll never get married."
To my dad I said these words, "I'll never settle down.
Got a need for roaming, don't want to get tied down."

But I've learned never say, "Never!"
No matter what you think
It's a bitter cup of words I'm gonna have to drink
Never say never, oh, listen to my plea
Or you'll have to drink from the same cup as me.

Soon we'll break the news about what I said would never be
I fell in love and it's happening to me
We're gonna marry, gonna try to settle down
This is the life I want, happiness I have found.[1]

Looking back over the past few decades, I am so very grateful that God had mercy on me and allowed me to enjoy being married to the best man in the whole world.

Even though I have a fierce determination to love my husband, to be honest with you, I'm still trying to figure out what love really is. And I get the feeling I'm not the only one. We live in a culture that is obsessed with the subject of love and relationships. Take a look at the cover of almost any woman's magazine. It seems that every article is about how to find the right man and then how to keep him happy. Or listen to the music on the radio. *Love.* Songs praise it. Movies dramatize it. Poets extol it. Teenagers exploit it. Old people eulogize it. Madison Avenue sells it. Churches proclaim it. Some even worship it. While everyone is talking about love, very few actually know what it really is.

What Does "Love" Mean?

Before we go any further with the discussion of how to love our husbands the way God intended, let's first do a little word study on "love." While the English language uses the word "love" for lots of things and in lots of ways, the Greek language, in which the New Testament was originally written, is much more specific. There are four different words used with four different meanings. Even though there are four words for love, only three of those words are ever used in the Bible.

The first Greek word for love is *eros*. This was the Greek term for sexual love. The root of this word is where we get "erotic." This word referred to sensual, carnal impulses to satisfy or gratify the sexual desires of the flesh. It shares a common root with the word *erao*, which means to ask, to beg, or to demand. Instead of a giving type of love, *eros* demands, it is a taking kind of desire. It does not seek to give pleasure, but to grab it for the self. When I was a young girl I heard the saying, "Love can always wait to give, but lust cannot wait to take." This self-satisfying, self-gratifying, self-seeking, self-pleasing type of sexual expression is not the kind of love any believer should permit in their marital relationship. By the way, this is the word for love that is never used in the Bible.[2]

The second Greek word for love is *stergo*. This word is primarily used to describe the love that exists between family members. One scholar noted that on occasion, the word *stergo* portrayed the love of a nation for its ruler. This word has even been used to picture the love of a dog for its master.[3]

The third word for love is *phileo*. This word describes affection such as the affection between a boyfriend and girlfriend. It is the genial feeling shared between two friends. It carries the idea of two or more people who feel compatible, well-matched, well-suited, and complementary to each other. It is from the word *phileo* that we get Philadelphia—brotherly love, philanthropic—love for mankind, and philosophy—love of wisdom.[4]

Eros, stergo, and phileo are the low-levels of love. To sum it up, *eros* is a self-seeking love. *Stergo* is limited to one's family and is the love that is behind the saying "Blood is thicker than water." *Phileo* love is based on mutual satisfaction. It's the kind that can yield feelings of disappointment when expectations are not met. While this is love, it is definitely conditional. In other words, "I will love you as long as you meet my expectations." Many marriages are based on this kind of love, and that is often why so many fail.

The kind of love that God demonstrates toward us and the kind of love He expects us to give to each other is *agape* love. This is the most common word for love in the New Testament. No Bible verse says it so well as John 3:16: "For God so loved the world that He gave His only begotten Son, that whoever believes in Him should not perish but have everlasting life" (NKJV). What does this verse mean?

God looked upon the human race. He loved mankind, even after man was lost in sin. Even though mankind was held captive by Satan at the fall, God looked upon the world and saw His own image. The human race was precious to God, and He loved man so deeply that His heart was stirred to reach out and do something to save him.[5] It's been said, "You can give without loving, but you cannot love without giving." *Agape* love demands action.

It is a sobering thought that God demands that we *agape* one another, even as He loves us. Oh what love! God offered redeeming love to a people who didn't deserve it, was not aware of His enormous sacrifice, and was totally unable to repay such a gift. It is this kind of love that He calls us as wives to give to our husbands and, conversely, that husbands are to give to their wives.

On a human level, what does that love look like? *Agape* love...

- knows no boundaries
- has no strings attached
- gives with no expectation of receiving anything in return
- sacrifices, regardless of whether that sacrifice is acknowledged or appreciated
- will do whatever it takes to see that the other's needs are met with no thought of self

- is patient in difficult circumstances
- is kind to all people
- builds up the other person
- exercises humility by not bragging of personal achievements
- is courteous
- is easygoing
- doesn't hold a grudge
- leaves no room in the heart for jealousy
- does not entertain thoughts of envy
- hates sin, but loves the sinner
- loves the truth and can quickly recognize a lie
- supports the other person
- always believes the best
- never gives up hope
- never gives in to evil
- never fails

When I look at what God's kind of love requires of me, I know loving this way is not humanly possible. But that's where God comes in. He will help us love this way. What does agape love look like in our daily lives? Here's a lyric that shows a giving and self-sacrificing love.

Feels Like Love

He knew all along it was one of her dreams
So he put a quarter in the music machine.
He took her hand and said, "You know I can't dance.
But darling just for you I'm gonna take that chance."

And she said, "Oh, baby, I can't believe it's true.
I never thought I'd be dancing with you.
Oh, baby, thank you so much. It might look like dancing,
But it feels like love. It might look like dancing, but with you
It feels like love."

And now it's Sunday in the afternoon.
She knows what he's doing in the TV room.
Watching cars go round in circles ain't her cup of tea
But she says, "Turn it up, scoot over, darling.
Make some room for me."

And he says, "Oh, baby, I can't believe it's true.
I never thought I'd watch racing with you.
Oh, baby, thank you so much.
Might look like racing, but it feels like love.
Might look like racing but with you, it feels like love."

Now, he's learned some moves, he's not afraid anymore
She smiles when they glide across that hardwood floor.
And there's a place down in Bristol, where she likes to be.
Sittin' next to her man who's wearing number three.[6]

Well, what do you think? Does that sound like love to you? Actually, what you just read in Steve's song is a modern picture of the ancient truth about *agape* love found in Philippians 2:2-4: "Make my joy complete by being of the same mind, maintaining the same love, united in spirit, intent on one purpose. Do nothing from selfishness or empty conceit, but with humility of mind regard one another as more important than yourselves; do not merely look out for your own personal interests, but also for the interests of others." Verse five goes on to describe Jesus Christ as the perfect example of *agape* love. We are instructed to have the same attitude in us that was in Jesus. What attitude would that be? The heart and the mindset of a servant who was willing to give up everything, holding nothing back, for the good of humankind.

I don't know about you, but I rarely see *agape* encouraged. It's definitely not the usual kind of love presented on the movie screens. It's seldom ever the kind of love proposed in romance novels or magazine articles. No, God's kind of love doesn't always make us feel comfortable. Of course it's great to be on the receiving end of that kind of love. But to give to another person with no expectations of receiving anything in return, I don't know about that. To sacrifice without acknowledgment or appreciation, is that realistic? Is it even smart to make ourselves so exposed, so open to being hurt by giving love so freely? Isn't that kind of overt love dangerously close to becoming a doormat for someone to abuse and use? To a lot of folks in our time, devotion such as *agape* love sounds too risky, too vulnerable, too meek, and downright naïve.

Is that really the kind of love God requires of us? Yes! Do I love like that? Not most of the time. *But I want my husband to know that my goal is to love him with God's kind of love—with* agape *love.*

The closest I've ever come to loving another human with that kind of love was when I was taking care of my babies. I served and sacrificed for Nathan and Heidi, knowing they didn't understand my acts of kindness. I'm sure there have been times when they thought I was being mean and unloving to them even when I was doing what was best for them. Perhaps when I took them to the doctor and they got shots, and were pricked and probed by some stranger in a white jacket, they didn't understand that love sometimes means that we allow momentary pain. But because of my great love for them I was willing to endure their wrath. Love sometimes demanded that I do what they needed, not necessarily what they wanted. Did my children thank me for all I did for them? No. Not at the time, anyway. Love gives with no expectations in return.

My heart aches when I think of the many ways love has been distorted. Every day men and women give their bodies over to demanding and demeaning sexual appetites and call it love. Young girls subject themselves to unplanned pregnancies, all sorts of sexually transmitted diseases, and emotional devastation that they will carry for the rest of their lives, trying to prove to pimpled-face adolescent boys that they love them. Emotionally starved individuals will choose perversion trying to find anything that remotely looks like love, even if it means sacrificing their bodies and souls. In the name of love, elderly folks compromise godly morals and standards, living together without the sanction of holy matrimony in order to keep from losing retirement benefits and avoid being alone.

Yes, love "takes it on the chin" when we use it to excuse all manner of ill behavior. One day I came across a list of definitions of love that were apparently written by little children. In their few years on earth, it seems they had found more truth in what love really looks like than some of us who have lived a full lifetime. Here are a few of their thoughts.

What Does Love Look Like?

- When someone loves you, the way they say your name is different. You know that your name is safe in their mouth. Billy, age 4

- Love is when a girl puts on perfume and a boy puts on cologne, and they go out and smell each other.

- Love is what makes you smile when you're really tired. Karl, age 5

- Love is what's in the room with you at Christmastime if you stop opening presents and listen. Bobby, age 5

- Love is when your puppy licks your face even after you left him alone all day. Mary Ann, age 4

- Love is when mommy sees daddy all smelly and sweaty and says he's handsomer than Robert Redford. Chris, age 8

- When my grandmother got arthritis, she couldn't bend over and paint her toenails anymore. So my grandfather does it for her all the time even after his hands got arthritis too. Rebecca, age 8

When I read the definitions of love through the eyes of these children, it doesn't seem so complicated. Love is giving what the other one needs. While love will certainly evoke feelings in us, it is not merely an emotion. No, love is indeed a verb. It's what we do.

How Can I Get Love Back?

Are you hesitant to love your husband with *agape* love? Some wives are asking the same question that was on the heart of a young husband who came to our house for a visit one late afternoon. He looked like he had not slept in days. He had a scared, unsure look in his eyes. He came to us at the bidding of his mother, who was an acquaintance of ours.

As he began to tell his story, I could have told it for him. How many times have we heard the same sad rendering of how apathy, lack of communication, and basic unloving, bad attitude had driven a wedge between spouses? This young man's lack of love pierced his wife's heart. His ways had pushed her over the edge, and now she was gone. Sadly, she was not the only one he had lost. She took their two little children and moved back to her mother's home. Now the man who had been so busy with everything and everyone but her could think of nothing else but winning his wife back. She finally had his attention. But was it too late?

Trying to help him see what he needed to do, we took this young man to the passage in Luke 18:35. In this account we read about Jesus coming into the city of Jericho. There was a man named Bartimaeus sitting along the side of the road begging. Why was he begging? That was his occupation. Bartimaeus was blind, and the only thing he could do to make a living was to sit and beg. Perhaps he had no family that could financially support him. He was left to depend on the pity and the piety of those who would drop him a coin.

When Bartimaeus heard the commotion, he began to call out to those around him, asking what was happening. They told him that Jesus was passing by. Somewhere along the way, Bartimaeus must have heard that Jesus was a man who could help people like him. With Jesus as his hope, the sad beggar cried out, "Jesus, Son of David, have mercy on me!"

Those around him sternly told Bartimaeus to hush. However, the more they shushed him the louder he became. "Jesus, Son of David, have mercy on me!"

When Jesus heard his call for help, He stopped and commanded that Bartimaeus be brought to Him. Then Jesus did something surprising. He asked Bartimaeus a question: "What do you want Me to do for you?"

Because it was quite obvious what the poor man needed, it seems strange that Jesus would ask such a question. Yet Jesus was asking the man to be specific, to tell Him exactly what he wanted Him to do. So Bartimaeus made his request very clear: "I want to regain my sight." In this statement he revealed that at one time he was able to see. Something had happened that caused him to lose his sight. What was Jesus' response to his very specific request? He said, "Receive your sight back." Jesus answered his precise cry for help.

In our den that late afternoon, we asked that neglectful-but-desperate husband, "What *exactly* do you want Jesus to do for you?" He said, "I want my wife back, and I want to love her like I once did."

Perhaps that's where you are. You may have loved your spouse dearly at one time, but now some of those feelings have evaporated. As you read the following lyric, can you relate to what that young man was feeling that day?

That Way Again

I want to feel love again,
Just like I did, way back when
We realized we were more than friends
I want to feel love that way again.

I want to hear our old song again
Just like I did way back then
Oh, how we'd sway while that record would spin
I want to hear our old song that way again

If love has faded, the fault is mine
I once could see but now I'm blind
I was the one who hid the view
Oh, Christ who heals, I come to You

I want to see that smile again
The one that told me way back then
My only love has just walked in
I want to see that smile that way again.[7]

Love Is a Verb

How do we get back what we have lost? How do we feel the way we once felt? There is actually an easy answer to that loaded question. *In order to feel the way we once felt, we must do the things we once did.* Do you remember some of things you did when you were in the process of winning your spouse? Did you spend a lot of time talking to one another? Did you seek out places and times so the two of you could be alone? Did you invest money, time, and effort in making sure the other one felt loved and treasured? Were you willing to move heaven and earth to keep your promises? Were you careful with the tiniest of details required to foster a pleasant environment? Did you attend to such things as personal hygiene? Did you diet and exercise in order to make sure your body was in shape and attractive? Have you stopped doing important things such as these?

When we win our spouses with one kind of behavior and then change the rules after the marriage vows are spoken, we have practiced deception. We have essentially lied to our beloveds. One young fellow told me that when he was dating his wife, she would go hunting with him. No morning was too cold; no hour was too early; no hill too steep to climb. Wherever he went hunting, she was there at his side. Now, eight years and a couple of kids later, she has no interest in going out in the cold while it's still dark to hunt down and kill some helpless little animal. What happened? To be fair, when children come along someone has to stay behind and take care of them. This is a justifiable reason to bow out of an activity. However, she stopped going with him long before the children came. It seems that in the beginning of their relationship she was willing to do whatever it took to win the heart of her intended. It's as though she was in a competition, as if she was running a race and the finish line was the marriage altar.

In the case of this "hunting couple," when I asked the wife if her husband had changed since they were dating, she had her own complaints. She was not the only one who changed the rules in the middle of the game. When they were dating he didn't want to sit at home on a Friday night and watch *Law and Order* reruns. No, he was excited to go out with her and spend time alone. He was the one who wanted to go out to eat or go to a movie. If she wanted to go shopping, he was right at her side. And visiting her mother on Sunday afternoons was a sheer delight…back then. She said it seemed as though when he repeated the vows he said, "Till the wedding do us part" instead of "till death do us part."

The reasons for the changes that happen from dating to married life are understandable. Very often there is more money for entertainment before children come along. When kids are in the picture instead of arranging for and paying a babysitter, it's easier to open a can of soup or throw a frozen pizza in the oven instead of going out to eat. Perhaps prior to children there was more energy, but now there's regular work as well as overtime to pay for braces, private schools, and to pay off the purchases made on credit cards.

Do things change over time? Of course they do. However it's not too late. You don't have to accept the sad possibility that you will have to live the rest of your married life without passion, without intimacy, feeling you are the only one in the world who is so unloved. My friend, you don't have to lose your feelings of love for one another. You can still make your spouse feel adored, cherished, and valued.

In the remaining chapters of this book we will explore the ways we can show *agape* love to our husbands. We want our husbands to know that we will love them fully, with no expectations, no boundaries, no strings attached. We want them to know that we intend to show that kind of love to them every day as long as we live. Each of us wants to love our spouse with *agape* love, demonstrated by:

- acknowledging his leadership and God-ordained headship in our home

- enthusiastically making myself available to him sexually

- showing my appreciation to him as a godly father and parenting partner

- supporting him as the financial provider and together building financial security for our family

- expressing my profound respect for him as a person, husband, father, and Christian brother

- encouraging him to find hobbies and friends that will contribute to his life and the good of our family

- making our home a safe harbor, a soft place for him to enjoy coming home to each day

- including and embracing his family as my very own and showing them the same respect and honor I show my family

- maintaining a high level of physical health and attractiveness so together we can live a long, fruitful life.

Don't worry. No one loves perfectly except God. As we go through this book we'll discuss ways we can show our spouses we love them. You'll be amazed at how deep and fulfilling your marriage can be!

2

I Want My Husband to Know

I Acknowledge Him as the God-Appointed Leader of Our Family

ONE OF THE MOST CONTROVERSIAL subjects, both in and out of the church, is the biblical teaching that states God has appointed the husband to be the head of the home. While it is indeed a doctrine that can be found in the Scriptures, sadly some extreme interpretations of the teaching have yielded resistance to the idea. I can remember in the late 1970s there was a major Christian denomination that declared that the doctrine of submission in marriage was to be unquestionably accepted and stringently practiced by married *female* members.

The problem was that the spirit of the teaching lacked the elements of grace and tenderness. Consequently, the response of many women was determined resistance. There was nearly an audible scream of protest that reverberated across the denominational landscape. Many wondered how a modern-day organization could adhere to such an archaic, out-of-step enforcement of the teaching. Some viewed the push toward such an extreme version of submission as paramount to taking away a woman's right to vote.

The questions that arose in a lot of women's minds, including mine, were: "What is the truth, and where is the balance in regard to the role of the husband's headship and the woman's submission in marriage? Is the husband supposed to 'rule the roost' and make all the decisions?"

I understand the conflict over this issue. When I was a young woman I regarded "submission" as an abomination. Even though I became a Christian in my young adulthood and had a sincere desire to be a woman who followed Christ and who obeyed the Bible, the idea of submission was not easy to accept. To be quite candid, I had a rather independent nature and the thought of submitting to a man didn't set well at all. Very simply, I didn't like being told what to do—no one does. And to add to the conflict, I had never met a man I deemed worthy of what I perceived as blind devotion and obedience.

The social tone of the times fueled the fire of my self-reliant attitude. Being born in 1951 and coming into my young adult years in the mid-70s, I was significantly influenced by many of the ideas of the feminist movement. The resounding motto of the era was "a woman needs a man like a fish needs a bicycle."

Even though I was sure that my mind was made up about the issue, I couldn't shake the conviction in my heart that I needed to come to grips with the teachings about submission in the Bible. The thought of ignoring just one portion of The Book that I deeply cherished (even if I didn't always agree with it) was too troublesome. So I began a journey of research regarding the teaching of submission. Using the book of 1 Peter, chapter 3 as the main text, it didn't take long until I began to see that I could be a strong, intellectually honest woman and still obey God's Word about being submissive to my husband. I found, to my surprise, an excitement about the concept of submission that I never expected to discover.

Are you grappling with wifely submission? Well, I have some good news. Submission is not our enemy, and neither is it a life sentence of being a second-class part of the marriage union.

Before I share with you how I came to accept the biblical application of submission in my marriage, let me first address a concern that has been expressed by some who believe that God has a bias against women. There are those who are convinced that Christianity is an oppressive, repressive religion designed to keep women bare-foot, unemployed, pregnant, and under the thumb of patriarchal man. Even though I understand how some could feel this way, their perception of Christianity could not be further from the truth.

First of all, the historical evidence testifies that the Christian faith is not and has never been a socially repressive religion that subjugates and oppresses women. In fact, the evidence shows quite the opposite. Whenever the truths of Christianity are introduced into a culture, the end result is one of enlightenment and liberation for both men and women.

At the time of the writing of the first epistle of Peter, the pre-Christian world was not only morally corrupt, but many barbaric, abhorrent practices were commonly accepted as the norm. Large numbers of people lost their lives through murder, abortion, infant exposure, and war. And sad to say, in those countries where Christianity is rejected today, things have not changed that much. In many parts of the world morally bankrupt systems still exist with little or no regard to the sacredness of life. However, societies that embraced the introduction of Christianity were often radically changed in very positive ways. This was accomplished because there were godly men and women serving as missionaries of the good news of Christ who were willing to clash with cultural norms. With great sacrifice of their own comfort and safety, they fought for the liberation and deliverance of the weak and helpless.

Two glowing examples of the brave souls who altered societies by delivering Christ to a nation were William and Catherine Booth. These founders of the Salvation Army worked to change the age of consent for young girls who were being prostituted. During the 1800s the Booths uncovered the widespread practice of selling young English girls into prostitution. Innocent girls were enticed to London with promises of a better life. There they were chloroformed, violated, and eventually trafficked into the white-slavery trade. The laws in Britain at the time protected the criminals who preyed upon these children. If the children were younger than 13, they could not take an oath to testify against their abductors. And if the children were over 13 they were considered within the age of consent. In the name of Jesus Christ, the Booths worked to change the laws to protect children who were being exploited by greedy, godless individuals.

In addition to the work of the Booths, there were Christian missionaries in Africa who discouraged polygamy, who fought against the slave trade, who built schools and hospitals for people of all faiths. It was the Christian missionaries in China who helped to enlighten people of the shame and abuse of wrapping little girls' feet, which crippled them for life. No other religion has done so much for so many.

The more I learned about the liberating effects that the Good News of Jesus Christ can have on a culture, the more I realized that the message I had believed from the militant feminists was a lie. The teachings of Christ did not promote the suppression and control of women. I say without reservation, anyone who regards Christianity as repressive and an enemy of women simply doesn't know or will not accept the facts. Without question, history bears out when a people embrace the teachings of Christ and the truths of the Bible are obeyed, they are set free. They experience true liberation—and that especially includes women.

Now, there have been those who have knowingly misused God's Word to lord it over their fellow human beings. All we have to do is look at our own country. There were selfish people who used God's Word to justify the institution of slavery for their own economical gain. Shamelessly they used a couple of Bible verses taken out of context and justified their racism and cruelty. If they had read and understood the full truth of God's Word, they could never have treated another human being in such an unloving, evil manner.

In the same way, when we understand the truth of God's Word and live according to it, we will learn that the concept of submission is not something men should use like a whip to control their wives. And God's Word was never meant to justify unkind and domineering behavior over another.

The Foundation of Submission

In chapters one and two of the first epistle of Peter, the apostle teaches us the pattern of how we are to conduct ourselves. It is important to keep in mind that the people Peter wrote to were Christians who had been scattered throughout the region because of their conversion to Jesus Christ. As a result of following Christ, many of them had lost their family inheritance, forfeited their relationships with family members, and suffered great physical peril. It is in this setting that Peter gives his fellow brethren instruction on how to live in a culture that was very hostile to their belief in Christ.

The recurring theme throughout the beginning chapter of 1 Peter is one of humility. Voluntarily submission to civil authorities, submission of employee to employer, and submission within the structure of the home are directed without apology.

To understand how confusing it must have been to the people Peter wrote to about submitting to civil authorities, consideration must be given to who was in power at the time. It was an Emperor by the name of Nero. Nero came from a lineage of unquestionable evil. His father was credited for many murders, and his mother poisoned his stepfather and later married Claudius. Persuading the emperor to designate Nero, her son, in place of his own as successor, she murdered Claudius before he could change his mind.

Nero came to power at the age of 16, and the legacy of evil continued with him. He either personally killed or had many of his wives killed. He murdered his mother. When Rome burned for a week in July A.D. 64, it was rumored that he had set fire to the city to make room for a new palace. When Christians refused to bow to him, he charged them with arson and "hatred of the human race." To divert the attention away from his own political problems, and for his own amusement, he had Christians arrested, tortured, and used as human torches to light his garden. Finally the Roman Senate declared him a public enemy and sentenced him to death by flogging. He escaped this sentence by committing suicide.

With crazed leaders like Nero in place, the people must have felt totally bewildered when Peter said that they were to submit to the civil authorities. How could Peter be justified in instructing these suffering Christians to be submissive to such a corrupt government? It was because he knew that no one came to a place of authority outside the sovereign will of God. Perhaps Peter was remembering the response that Jesus gave when Pilate asked Him at His precrucifixion trial, "Do You not know that I have authority to release You, and I have authority to crucify You?" And Jesus answered, "You would have no authority over Me, unless it had been given you from above" (John 19:10-11).

The concept of submission should not be a surprise to anyone who seeks to pattern his or her life after Christ. In 1 John 2:5-6 we are told, "By this we know that we are in Him: the one who says he abides in Him ought himself to *walk in the same manner as He walked.*" How did Jesus walk? He submitted Himself to the Father. In the garden of Gethsemane He cried out to God concerning the cruel death that awaited Him. He prayed, "My Father, if this cannot pass away unless I drink it, Your will be done" (Matthew 26:42). Even in the triune God-head there is submission. John 17:4 reports that Jesus said to the heavenly Father, "I glorified You on the earth, having accomplished the work which You have given Me to do." Jesus also revealed in John 5:19, "The Son can do nothing of Himself, unless it is something He sees the Father doing; for whatever the Father does, these things the Son also does in like manner." Following His example, we must understand that humility and submission are not the exception to the rule. They are the norm.

Peter summed up how we should conduct ourselves in 1 Peter 2:17: "Honor all people, love the brotherhood, fear God, honor the king." He went on to instruct the servants to obey their masters when it came to their work, whether the master was good and gentle or unreasonable. Humility was and is to be the hallmark of every true believer.

Submission Is an Opportunity

With the backdrop of his instruction in chapter 2 about being submissive to both the civil authorities and employers, Peter then turns his attention to the believer's home life. In the opening words in chapter 3 the wives are the first to be instructed: "In the same way, you wives, be submissive to your own husbands so that even if any of them are disobedient to the word, they may be won without a word by the behavior of their wives."

The key transitional phrase in the verse is "In the same way . . ." Looking back to chapter 2, it is clear that when submission is offered to civil authorities, ultimately that submission is to God, not necessarily to man. In the same way, as a woman submits to her husband, her act of humility is ultimately toward God. Let me illustrate.

My husband, Steve, and I are musicians. We sang and worked together 24/7 for the first couple years of our marriage. In 1976 we found out that we would be adding to our family. After I learned that I was pregnant with our son, I began to pray about the changes taking place in my life. What was I suppose to do as a soon-to-be mother? I felt God impress on me that I was free to leave the singing group Steve and I were in. I eagerly accepted this new calling and told Steve I needed to remain home with our child.

For the next few months I continued to travel until alternative arrangements could be made to replace me. Steve and his singing partner employed a five-piece band to take my place. (I like to think it took five men to do my job!) So when my son, Nathan, was nine months old, I stopped traveling with the group. The addition of the band was a great asset to the sound and appeal of the group, and I was pleased that their expanding concert schedule reflected that. However, as good as they sounded there was one downside to taking on a multimember band. Suddenly the number of mouths that had to be fed grew from two families to seven. Consequently, it became necessary for the group to travel 21 or more days a month.

Although the ministry Steve and the fellows were involved in had noticcable results, the continuous traveling began to take its toll on our family. The decision to make a change became much easier for Steve after an incident between him and our then nearly three-year-old son, Nathan.

Steve returned home after three weeks of concerts. Not long after he got home, Nathan did something he wasn't supposed to do. Steve, wanting to be the dutiful daddy, reprimanded him for his misbehavior. Neither Steve nor I realized what his traveling had done to Nathan's perception of the role of a father. After being disciplined by a man Nathan essentially considered to be an occasional visitor, our little boy stuck his little finger in Steve's face and said, "Old man, why don't you get in that motorhome and take another trip."

To this day we are both extremely grateful that through Nathan we were able to see that there was a problem. It's scary to think how easily we could have missed the signs that our son was in trouble. It was after the "motorhome incident," as it became known in our family, that Steve began making arrangements to leave the band and stop traveling.

For the six months following his decision to "come home" Steve was busy not only fulfilling his contractual responsibilities with the band but also earnestly praying about what he was going to do. He soon became convinced that the two of us were to start working together as we once had done. Only this time it would be just our family. He was convinced that we could take the children with us and minister together as a couple.

When Steve presented this idea to me, I was adamantly opposed to it. Traveling and singing with our little family, which by now included our infant daughter, Heidi, along with a three-year-old, seemed impossible. There was no way I wanted to pack up two babies and start traveling all over the country. I encouraged Steve to go by himself; there was no way I was going along with him.

Are you wondering how this account fits into the idea of how a wife's submission to her husband is ultimately her service to God? There's more. It would not be unreasonable for you to think this is where Steve took out the Bible and showed me the verses about submission. And it would be understandable if you assumed that he reminded me that he was the head of the home and I was to obey him. For some couples that might be exactly what would have happened. However, not in this case, and I will be forever grateful for it.

After Steve expressed his desire for us to work together and I gave him my "No way, Bubba!" look, he never mentioned it again. He didn't try talking me into it. He didn't tell me I was being a bad wife by not submitting to him. He didn't even leave the Bible open for me to find Colossians 3:18: "Wives, be subject to your husbands, as is fitting in the Lord." He didn't remind me of Ephesians 5:22: "Wives, be subject to your own husbands, as to the Lord. For the husband is head of the wife." He didn't tell me God was displeased with me for my obstinate attitude. He didn't even tell me what a positive experience it would be for our little family to be together. Instead, after I said no with my words and my facial expression, he dropped the subject. At least that's what I thought he did.

Since I thought the idea was so totally ridiculous, I never gave it another thought. But I didn't know Steve was fervently praying about us working together. A few weeks after our brief discussion, Steve had to leave for a weeklong trip. It was during his absence that I started having a recurring dream.

To my horror, I dreamed that I was an unfaithful wife. *Whew! Where did that come from?* I wondered. I was troubled by the dream. What could have caused me to imagine such a thing? Had I watched a movie with adultery as a theme? No. Had I talked about someone who had been unfaithful to her husband? No.

The next night when I went to sleep, I dreamed the exact same thing. This went on for six straight nights. By the seventh day I was not only exhausted in my body from a lack of restful sleep, but I was extremely disturbed in my soul and spirit. Through the week I cried out to the Lord, "What is in me that I would dream such a dream? Are you showing me that I have an unfaithful heart? Could I be that wicked and be unaware of it?"

Finally, on the seventh day when I was desperate for an answer, the Lord whispered something in my heart: "You are an unfaithful wife because you won't do what I have called you to do. I want you to sing with Steve."

All of a sudden the question of my nonsubmissive attitude was not between Steve and me. My clash with submission became an issue of disobedience between my Maker and me. It became very obvious that I had a decision to make. Not too long after that Steve and I packed up our "young'uns," and we hit the road. Now, looking back over these many years of traveling with our children from colic to college, I'm glad I obeyed the Lord and submitted to Steve. I have no regrets. We have enjoyed a wonderful life together. We've met the best people all around the country. We've sung for notable dignitaries in the Christian community. And we've enjoyed opportunities we never dreamed possible.

Has the road always been easy? Of course not. There were many times while traveling with children that I wanted to quit. We experienced the full span of emotions traveling as a family. We potty-trained and homeschooled our kids from sea to shining sea. We dealt with everything from the rolling of the eyes of disappointed teens who sacrificed so many of their own social experiences to enjoying working with them as young, beautiful, and responsible adults. Without question I wouldn't trade one minute of our time together. Okay, maybe there were a few days I wouldn't mind losing track of. But that's part of life.

One memory I could do without is the day one of the kids got food poisoning in New Mexico. Steve and I stayed up all night with Heidi as she splattered our hotel room with 14 (we counted them) episodes of vomiting. We said a special prayer for the unfortunate cleaning person who was assigned to clean the room.

While we've stayed in some very nice hotels, we unfortunately stayed in a Texas motel that left us with flea bites all over our bodies. We've stayed in homes that were veritable mansions, but we have also slept on cold floors and even once slept in a laundry room surrounded by baskets of dirty clothes. We've been in planes that nearly crashed. We've been stranded away from home during snowstorms and tornadoes. And at least once we were forced to visit the emergency room in an unfamiliar town when one of the children fell at a swimming pool and required a head full of stitches.

There's no doubt that if Steve had talked me into our life of traveling I would have blamed him for many things that went wrong when the going got tough. But because he submitted his request to God, and God worked in my heart to go, I didn't blame Steve when I was unhappy with my circumstances. Even though submission looks like a made-for-man idea, it really is what makes the Christian life authentic, especially as a wife.

Even though the concept of submission was once so foreign and repulsive to me, I now embrace it with great joy. Why the extreme turn-a-round? Over the years I've come to understand that what starts out as an obligation to submit actually turns into an opportunity to see God's order in the home. I am aware that if I first submit out of a love and respect for God, that act of obedience becomes a great chance to show love and respect for my husband.

One day something happened that reminded me again of the truth of submission. While I was cleaning the garage a little hummingbird flew in. It was easy for him to make his way in, but he was finding it impossible to figure his way out. I tried everything I could think of to help him out. My time window was closing, and I needed to close the garage door and leave. I knew if I closed the little bird up in the garage he would probably die due to a lack of food and water.

The only thing I could think of was to take a broom and hold it up close to him with the hope that the little bird would land on it and then I could gently lower it down to the outside so the creature could find its freedom. It was very frustrating. The more I tried to help him, the more he shrunk back from me. I'm sure he must have seen the broom and thought I was trying to kill him. He didn't see it as a means of freedom; he must have thought it was an instrument of hurt. But the broom was the only way he could get to freedom. Submission is like that broom. It is not an instrument of harm. Instead, it is the very thing that can help us get where we need to go and have what we want to have.

Contrary to what some may assume, submission does not mean being void of an opinion. Neither does it mean blindly obeying a husband. To grasp this truth, it is important to know there are two different words for submission in the original Greek, the language the Bible is written in. This will help us understand what God requires of us.

One word for submitting is the word *kathos*. That word means to obey like a slave obeys a master or like a child obeys a parent. That *is not* the word used in the 1 Peter 3 passage. The one used there is *homois*. This means to "serve with a positive motive for the Lord's sake, to voluntarily serve out of a willing spirit."

Biblical submission has nothing to do with being enslaved, coerced, or dominated by force. Neither does it have anything to do with a "superiority verses inferiority" battle. It has everything to do with our homes functioning in God's divine order.

Our role and position as a wife is described in the book of Genesis. When God created Eve He said He was making her for the purpose of being a suitable helper for her husband. That is not to say that women were an afterthought of God. No, He knew from the beginning that women would be essential to fulfill His plan for mankind. From the beginning, husbands and wives were designed to work together. An example that vividly illustrates this is taken from the wonderful world of horses.

One day I read about a horse-pulling contest. The winning horse pulled 4,500 pounds. The first runner-up pulled 4,000 pounds. But when harnessed together the two horses pulled over 12,000 pounds. When a team of horses work together, there is always a lead horse. What a wonderful illustration of God's plan for our homes. Husbands and wives are much stronger, more able, and much more profitable when they pull together. Submission makes this strong team possible. What would have happened if one of the horses in this contest had decided to go a different direction or if one had decided to not pull at all? The team effort would have been nullified.

Continuing with that analogy, when the wife decides to step out of the harness that is designed for two and pull in the opposite direction, the team suffers. Or if she decides her input is unimportant and she's going to let the husband do all the work of making decisions, the team suffers. Some women have the misconception that being submissive to their husbands consists of basically one response that is reflected in two words said mindlessly: "Yes, Dear." Sometimes those two words take different forms. When the husband asks her opinion the "yes, Dear" woman might answer, "Whatever you want, Honey," or "I don't know what we should do—you decide," or "I don't care, it's all up to you." And sometimes there's the really weak answer: "You're the boss. I'll do whatever you tell me to do."

Do you feel a little nausea coming on? I don't blame you. There is something very unattractive about an uninvolved wife who thinks she's obeying God by being submissive to her husband when in reality she's just being lazy or misguided. Submission is not passive. There is great responsibility when you're involved in a team, whether it be in a horse-pulling contest or a baseball game. In sports it's not just the captain of the team who does all the work and makes all the decisions. If the wife, as an essential team member, doesn't do her part, then the game will likely be lost. And when it comes to our homes, we can't afford such an outcome.

Ecclesiasties 4:9-12 states it very well. The New Living Translation puts it this way: "Two people can accomplish more than twice as much as one; they get a better return for their labor. If one person falls, the other can reach out and help. But people who are alone when they fall are in real trouble. And on a cold night, two under the same blanket can gain warmth from each other. But how can one be warm alone?"

Submitting to God's order in our homes makes us all stronger. The order designated by God is not about value or worth; but it has to do with function, productivity, and the preservation of the home. There is no question what that order is to be. First Corinthians 11:3 makes it clear: "Christ is the head of every man, and the man is the head of a woman, and God is the head of Christ." Notice that submission is part of *every* relationship.

Every well-functioning organization has to have a chain of command. In the workplace there are functions of responsibility. Just because the president of the company may have a position of authority, it doesn't make him a better person, nor even more valuable to the workplace than, say the vice president, the office manager, the electrician, or the maintenance man. If any of these individuals fails to do his job, the organization doesn't function to its fullest potential. One's position or office has nothing to do with that person's value or worth. In the same way, the home is a living organism. It is a living factory that works best with responsible people. Each member of the family must labor together.

Submission doesn't necessarily mean that the husband makes all the decisions or that all of his decisions are the best ones. It is not uncommon for Steve to submit to my ideas or direction. Ephesians 5:21 reminds us to "be subject to one another in the fear of Christ." More than once, for example, Steve has leaned on my talent for "horse trading," a skill I learned from watching my own father do it. When we have purchased replacement vehicles, Steve has willingly subjected himself to my handling of the deals, and it has saved us a lot of money through the years.

Submission as a Witness

True biblical submission is a powerful force for good. We read in 1 Peter 3 that it can actually win over an unbelieving, unyielding spouse. Peter was writing to the Christian women who were married to unbelieving husbands. I believe the women Peter wrote to were women who had come to faith in Christ after they were already married. In the Middle Eastern culture of the time it would have been extremely dangerous for the wife to try to overtly convert her husband to Christ. Women were not to be in authority over men, so trying to "teach" the husband most likely would not have been well received by him. Wisely, Peter instructed the wives that the best way to win their husbands to Christ was not by talking them into it, but by walking it out in front of them. There is something irresistible about seeing Christ-love demonstrated rather than listening to it illustrated.

Peter gives hope to the wives that their nonbelieving husbands might be won by the gentle and quiet spirit of submission. Keep in mind the intention of this passage is not to encourage women to submit to being physically hurt, emotionally brutalized, or made to do ungodly acts. God would never ask us to voluntarily agree to that kind of treatment or behavior. If that's your situation, seek help immediately.

God has put into our hands a wonderful tool to help us win an unbeliever to a life dedicated to the Lord. The apostle Peter tells us the most effective way to win an unbelieving spouse. He says, "Your godly lives will speak to them better than any words. They will be won over by watching your pure, godly behavior" (1 Peter 3:1 NLT). "Wordless" evangelism is by far the most difficult of all evangelism. However, *being a witness,* rather than giving one is the most effective. Do you want to win your husband to Christ? Try winning him not by your chatter, but by your character. Win him with your behavior not your blathering.

I've known women who were married to unbelieving husbands. Many of them tried all kinds of things to win them to Christ.

- Some would keep their radios tuned to Christian stations hoping their men would hear something over the airwaves that would touch their hearts.

- Some would leave pamphlets and Christian books all around the house with the hope their husbands might read something that would prompt a decision for Christ.

- Some would plead for their spouses to go to church or to special music concerts.

- We've had women bring their husbands to marriage seminars praying that the event would be the thing that would "break" them.

- Some would even put their children up to talking to their dads, even begging them to give their hearts to Jesus.

- Pastors have been invited over for the express purpose of talking to husbands about their souls.

- Some women try to "make" their husbands come to Christ. One woman, for example, said she was going to pray and fast until he became a Christian. Eventually she learned that not even God will "make" a person love and serve Him.

Many things are tried, and yes, some work. But often those overt attempts are met with hardened hearts and deaf ears. What are the most attractive ornaments a woman can wear to win the heart of her spouse? The apostle Peter tells us it is not beautiful clothes that adorn the outside. It is not the intricate hairdos or the fine gold jewelry that add sizzle and sparkle that get her spouse's attention. No, it is the imperishable qualities of a gentle and quiet spirit that are irresistible.

Think about the power of submission in this way: If God can use a quiet, gentle, submissive attitude to change the heart of a worldly, hardened, unregenerate man, how much more can a woman's kind, submissive behavior move the heart of a man who is already given over to God? There's enough hope in that thought for wives everywhere to rejoice!

3

I Want My Husband to Know

I Am Sexually Available to Him

THE DESIRE OF MY HEART is to meet my husband's needs in a holy and mutually satisfying way. I want our sexual relationship to be based on reciprocated respect. I never want to ask him to do anything that violates his conscience, nor do I want to be asked to do anything that violates mine. Together we can show honor toward God and fulfill His purpose for us as it pertains to physical intimacy.

God is not a prude. In fact, the sexual relationship between a husband and wife was part of God's creative plan from the beginning of time. Some may think that because sin entered into the world through the fall of Adam and Eve God hastily threw together a "plan B"—and came up with the idea of sex as a necessary evil needed to procreate the human race. Wrong! Nothing could be further from the truth.

All we have to do is take a peek at the way a man's and a woman's body fit together, and we will see the magnificent design of the sexual relationship. Of all the pictures that display God's creative handiwork, the intimacy and beautiful oneness that God designed for the crowning glory of His creation is one of the clearest. After He was finished speaking the world into existence, He stood back and declared, "It is good!" Among the many "good" things He proudly extolled were two very sexual beings who would use their sexual power to be fruitful and multiply after their own kind.

Not only does the practical compatibility of the male and female body parts display God's plan for sexuality, the very words of Jesus in Matthew 19:5 also lets us in on the original plan. These words were spoken when the religious leaders of the day came to Jesus, not to be taught by Him but to try to catch Him saying something they could use against Him. They asked, "Is it lawful for a man to divorce his wife for any reason at all?"

Jesus answered them and said, "Have you not read that He who created them from the beginning made them male and female, and said, 'For this reason a man shall leave his father and mother and be joined to his wife, and the two shall become one flesh?' So they are no longer two, but one flesh. What therefore God has joined together, let no man separate." The one flesh union Jesus is referring to in this passage addresses both the spiritual as well as the sexual union of marriage.

This union is considered most sacred, and for that reason, throughout Scripture, we are warned to protect ourselves from abusing our God-given sexuality. In 1 Corinthians 6:13-20 we read that we must be careful how we use our bodies and that sexual immorality carries a bonding of both flesh and spirit. Verses 16-20 say, "Do you not know that the one who joins himself to a prostitute is one body with her? For He says, 'The two shall become one flesh.' But the one who joins himself to the Lord is one spirit with Him. Flee immorality. Every other sin that a man commits is outside the body, but the immoral man sins against his own body....For you have been bought with a price: therefore glorify God in your body."

Do you see how important it is for a person to remain pure and avoid involving the body in sexual sin? First Thessalonians 4:3 says, "For this is the will of God, your sanctification; that is, that you abstain from sexual immorality." Why is God so concerned that we protect the powerful force of sexuality and keep it only for the context of marriage? Because it holds incredible bonding power.

Considering the power of the sexual relationship with our husbands, it is even more important that God's love govern our attitudes and behaviors.

As you may recall, there are four Greek words used for the word *love*. *Eros* is most often associated with sexual love. *Eros* is the root word for erotic, erotica and other such words that depict sexual arousal. Interestingly enough, *eros* is never used in the Bible to describe love. As you may recall, *eros* carries with it the idea of a demanding lust, of grabbing, and of a selfish taking for one's own pleasure. Since the beginning of time, God never intended sexual love to be a means for self-gratification. Instead, it is *agape* love—the love that seeks to please, to give, to fulfill—that God wants to be the motivator of our sexual relationship with our spouses.

The picture of this kind of *agape* love is found in the Philippians passage that states that other's needs should be regarded as more important than our own. When *agape* love dictates every interaction between a husband and wife, the sexual relationship is what it can and should be.

As wives, we should want our husbands to know that we intend to love them, including sexually, with God's kind of love. However, we must be aware that loving with *agape* love is not easy. That kind of love requires a lot of us. It calls us to give of ourselves, to serve. It asks us to do difficult things like bridle our tongues. But perhaps one of the most challenging things that *agape* loves asks us to do is to assume the best of our spouses.

For instance, on an isolated basis (not a pattern of behavior), has your husband ever assured you that he would be home at a certain time, only to show up much later? How did you react when that happened? Did you immediately assume he was trying to make your life more difficult? Did you presume he was attempting to sabotage dinner or deliberately make you late for your book club? When we live in *agape* love, we are obligated to assume the best. Perhaps he was delayed by heavy traffic or something else happened that caused him to be late.

In those times when assuming the best of a spouse is put to

test, instead of attacking with an emotional assault and personal insults, *agape* love calls for us to think more highly of our partner's intentions. Remember *agape* love gives mercy and grace with no expectations, no strings attached. Nothing can make a marriage more fulfilling than having *agape* love at the foundation.

Of course, God does not call just the wife to this great love. *Agape* love is gender neutral. When husbands and wives both treat each other with loving reactions and exercise a giving, selfless, other's-oriented response, then their marriages can be what God truly intended—a picture of how Christ loves the church. There will be no problem, no challenge, and no situation that cannot be overcome when *agape* love reigns supreme.

How does cultivating this kind of positive attitude toward a spouse influence the sexual love between a husband and a wife? Without question, our actions and attitudes outside the bedroom provide the fertile soil where love can grow. When we treat one another with respect, expecting the best from one another, then giving that wondrous *agape* love is not a dreadful chore but a grateful choice.

Are There Sexual Limits in Marriage?

Not long ago I talked to a number of young women who had recently gotten married. One common area of inquiry concerned their sexual relationships with their husbands. A recurring question was, "Is there anything that is off-limits when it comes to fulfilling my husband's sexual needs?"

Just the fact that some of the newlyweds were asking the question told me there was conflict about what was going on in their bedrooms. For instance, one young woman asked about the sexual fantasy games her husband wanted her to play. She felt demeaned by his need to pretend that she was someone other than his wife in order for him to be sexually aroused.

Without question a wife is responsible to meet her husband's sexual needs. And undeniably, she is the *one and only person* in the whole world who can honorably and righteously do so. However, there can be a big difference between meeting a legitimate need and fulfilling an unholy fantasy. Biblically, it is not a wife's duty to engage in a husband's lust-driven fantasies.

In defense of "anything goes in the bedroom," some have used Hebrews 13:4 as their argument. That passage says, "Marriage is to be held in honor among all, and the marriage bed is to be undefiled; for fornicators and adulterers God will judge." To twist this text to mean "because it is done in the bed of people who are married, whatever the act is can be assumed holy" is simply not what is intended. This scripture is a warning about not allowing adultery and fornication to enter a marriage bed, not a license to demand activities that are motivated by lewdness or that violate a spouse's conscience. In order to keep the marriage bed undefiled we must protect our relationship by living according to godly principles. The following suggestions may be helpful in living in purity within the bonds of marriage.

Renounce Premarital Sexual Involvement

God is not the only one who understands the power of the sexual union. The enemy of our souls, Satan himself, doesn't often wait until after the wedding day to attempt destruction of marriage. Instead, he usually starts long before the vows are said. One of the ways he will seek to destroy marital oneness is to convince a couple that it is permissible to be involved sexually outside of marriage. But it's not all right. Regardless of how socially acceptable it is these days to be sexually active and unmarried, it is still sin. It doesn't matter how many celebrities act like it's no big deal to live with one another without the commitment of marriage, it is still wrong.

Don't be deceived. Sin always exacts a terrible toll, and someone will pay the price. Unfortunately, in most cases it seems that the woman ends up paying the larger share of the bill, and the following true story is a sad representation of that fact.

A young, hormone-driven couple prayed about whether they should have sex outside of marriage. They held hands, bowed their heads and prayed, "Dear God, if you don't want us to have sex, make us have a flat tire on the way to the motel."

Since they arrived at the motel with all four tires inflated, they assumed God had made them the lone exception to His commands regarding holy living. They had sex. A few weeks later they were devastated when she found out she was pregnant. What was their response? They were mad at God. They had prayed about whether they should have sex, and since He didn't supernaturally knife one of their tires, they felt it was His fault that the little one was on the way.

Even though Steve and I knew that God's Word clearly tells us that we are to live free from sexual immorality, I am very grateful that God gave us a little extra warning about this temptation while we were dating. That warning came in the form of a dream Steve had. He would be quick to add that on the surface it may appear that getting the warning in such a way might make us look strong and in touch with God. However, in reality we were both so weak and vulnerable to temptation that God must have known we would hear His warning in no other way. Keep in mind that we were nearing our mid-twenties and ready to make up for lost time in regard to our physical appetites. In Steve's words, the story goes,

> I was careful about reading too much into dreams. I can eat pizza at night and have some really weird images pass through my head. But sometimes God does use dreams to show us something we need to know. And that's what God did in this case. He warned us both to protect our marriage bed, even before we made our vows to one another.
>
> In the dream, Annie and I were traveling from Nashville to the house where I was living in Franklin, Tennessee, before we married. I was driving, and it was a cold, wintry day. We were traveling south on I-65 out of Nashville in our old 1950 Chevy. Because of the cold weather, Annie reached through the steering wheel to turn up the heat, and when she pulled her arm back, a

big button on her coat sleeve got caught in the chrome of the steering wheel. She inadvertently ripped the steering wheel out of my hand, and we went off the road, down over a hill, and plowed through a fence. Right before we tore through the high chain-link fence we saw a sign that said, "NO TRESPASSING. KEEP OUT."

By the appearance of the very official-looking sign we had just seen, we knew we were on highly restricted property. We came to a standstill and sank into the thick, sticky mud up to the axle of the old Chevy. As we sat there in the silence, shaken to the core, we looked up on a hillside and our eyes were simultaneously drawn to a lovely sight. We visually feasted on one of the most beautiful houses either of us had ever seen. There was something very unusual about the house and its surroundings. Even though it was cold and wintry outside, the house was encircled with an array of glorious flowers. While everything else was bleak and chilly, it seemed to be summer there.

As we looked in awe at the home, I heard a voice speak to me about it, and the words were much more chilling than the wintry air. "That is the home I was leading you to, but because you have trespassed, you will not make it there."

My heart sank in disappointment and fear. I could remember feeling tears form in my eyes as I processed the sobering words I had just heard. I knew it was related to Annie's and my physical relationship. Then the silence was suddenly broken by the sound of sirens. The authorities rushed the car, pulled me off in one direction and Annie in another. Somehow we knew we would not be together again.

The morning after Steve had that dream he drove to Nashville to pick me up. When I got in the old car he began to tell me about it. The subdued sound of his voice told me he had had a troubled night. It didn't take a Ph.D. in Dreamology to figure out that God was telling us both something very important. We felt sufficiently warned to "stay away from the restricted property" of each other's bodies. From that moment on until we were married, we were both on guard to make sure we didn't mess up and miss out on what God had planned for us.

God's plan for protecting our future home by maintaining sexual purity was simple to understand but not easy to follow. We had to consciously guard against not being in a house together alone and not traveling by ourselves. We enlisted other ways to deliberately avoid putting ourselves in compromising situations. And add to that our constant, prayerful attitude before the Lord, seeking His help and strength to follow His order to remain pure before marriage. By the grace of God we made it to the altar without violating each other. And as a result, we can report that we have been enjoying our "dream home"—our wonderful life together—these many years since.

For some, the dating days were not a dream come true but more like an unending nightmare. What if you failed to remain pure before your vows were spoken? I know I don't have to tell you that sin has consequences. You're already very aware of that. Without a doubt, sin never unites; it always divides. So what should a couple do who has "stepped out of bounds" in the dating game? Does getting married fix the problem of premarital sexual involvement? Often couples think that a signed marriage certificate will somehow cancel out the sin problem. However, without confession and repentance of the sin of sexual immorality, the couple will simply bring that contamination into the marriage. Marriage is not a cure for lust.

What if you lived together outside the bonds of marriage? What if you and your husband had sexual relations while you were dating? What if you had a child outside of marriage? Can God bless your union even after you've done things that disobeyed His Word and broke His commandments? The answer is absolutely yes! Even those who never sexually touched one another before they got married have areas of their lives where they have sinned and transgressed against God and His Word. Yet despite our sinfulness, Jesus is full of mercy and full of compassion.

Hebrews 4:14 says,

> Since we have a great high priest who has passed through the heavens, Jesus the Son of God, let us hold fast our confession. For we do not have a high priest who cannot sympathize with our weaknesses, but One who has been tempted in all things as we are, yet without sin. Therefore let us draw near with confidence to the throne of grace, so that we may receive mercy and find grace to help in time of need.

It is with confidence, not in our own goodness for there is none, but in the fact that Jesus loves us and has pity on our weaknesses that we can go to Him. Thankfully, we can also lean on the comforting promise found in 1 John 1:9 that gently says, "If we confess our sins, He is faithful and righteous to forgive us our sins and to cleanse us from all unrighteousness."

One of my favorite sections of Scripture speaks of God's great love and mercy on those of us who have failed, even those who have failed miserably. That beautiful assurance of God's love is found in Psalm 103:8,10-14.

> The LORD is compassionate and gracious, slow to anger and abounding in lovingkindness....He has not dealt with us according to our sins, nor rewarded us according to our iniquities. For as high as the heavens are above the earth, so great is His lovingkindness toward those who fear Him. As far as the east is from the west, so far has He removed our transgressions from us. Just as a father has compassion on his children, so the LORD has compassion on those who fear Him. For He Himself knows our frame; He is mindful that we are but dust.

And those who have stumbled, especially in premarital tempta-tions, can find great hope in Micah 7:18-19:

> Who is a God like You, who pardons iniquity and passes over the rebellious act....He does not retain His anger forever, because He delights in unchanging love. He will again have compassion on us; He will tread our iniqui-ties under foot. Yes, You will cast all their sins into the depths of the sea.

I don't know about you, but when I read how much God loves us and is more than willing to forgive us when we confess and for-sake our sin, it makes me fall in love with Him even more!

God's love and forgiveness is boundless, even in the face of our failures. Here's a picture of His great love in a lyric Steve wrote about a dad who was faced with the disappointing news that his daughter became pregnant outside of marriage. This father had a particularly difficult time coming to grips with the fact that his little girl was going to have a baby out of wedlock. We watched as he struggled to embrace his daughter and the infant that grew within her. Though it wasn't easy, eventually he chose grace and mercy over hurt and judgment, and he led his family to show the daughter God's kind of love. The dad did not allow disappointment to steal compassion.

We Will Love This Child

We will love this child, my child.
That grows inside of you
Love is how God smiles
So love is what we'll do
A dream come true too early
Still can be a dream come true
We will love this child, my child,
The little one in you.

This was not my plan for you or me
But plans were made to change sometimes

If they have to be
This child will lead you on a journey
To a different place in time
But love will go there with you
And you will find
Yes, you will find that...

We will love this child, my child,
The little one in you.[1]

Whether your escapades before marriage bore the kind of evidence this young girl birthed or if it was done in secret, now is the time to ask God to cleanse your heart from the sin so that the complete joy of the sexual union can be restored. If there is an emotional wedge between you and your husband that is driven deeper by the hammer of guilt, Christ can remove it through confession of sin. I strongly urge you to pray for God's forgiveness and then discreetly approach your husband and ask him if he would be willing to verbalize a prayer of repentance about the sin of premarital physical involvement. (Sex doesn't have to be an "all the way" experience to be sinful.) If he is willing, perhaps the following short prayer would be useful. I suggest voicing this prayer in unison.

Dear God,

We come before you in Jesus' name, asking You to forgive us for our trespassing against one another physically before we married. Thank You for Your mercy and grace. Restore to us the joy of this part of our relationship. Help us to always be mindful that we should follow only Your guidelines when it comes to our physical union. Amen.

Refuse to Bring Others into the Bedroom

A few years ago we had some dear friends who were going through a heart-breaking situation. The husband had gotten involved in an adulterous affair at work. The wife and their five children were devastated, to say the least. We didn't know if the marriage was going to survive. But because of God's grace working in the forgiving spirit of the wife, it did. One of the saddest things the wife shared with me was the report about the night her husband began to suddenly cry. She actually felt relief because she thought he was feeling divine remorse for what he had done. She asked him what was wrong, and she was stunned when her husband answered, "I miss her so much."

I was truly impressed at how much grace this wife showed her wayward husband. While she made it very clear that she considered his behavior abhorrent and unacceptable, she also refused to love in any other way than with *agape* love. Her determination to keep God at the center of how she responded was the one thing that served most to restore the marriage that is still intact to this day.

Bringing others into the marriage relationship defiles the marriage bed in a serious way. Unfortunately, the sin of adultery is not the only sin that can defile a couple's relationship.

Refuse to Compare a Spouse with Others

One of the destructive factors in living a sexually promiscuous life is the loss of innocence. When Steve and I were married less than a year, I was talking to a friend who had gotten married a couple of months after we did. She confided in me that she was bored with her sexual relationship with her husband. I asked her how that could be since they had only been married a short time. She said, "I've had better sex with former lovers."

I believe we could call this an unintended consequence of living outside God's plan. Even though this couple remained married for a few more years, long enough to have four little children, they eventually divorced. You don't have to be a Dr. Phil to see that comparing a mate to other lovers is a main ingredient in the recipe for divorce. Every time we allow ourselves to think of other sexual experiences, we are undermining our marriage to our spouses. In a real sense, when we entertain thoughts of former sexual encounters there are other people in our marriage bed—and thus it is defiled.

Sometimes the other person(s) invited into the marriage bed are not remembrances of former lovers, but visual sexual images as a result of pornography. Pornography is anonymous adultery. It doesn't matter if the sexual partners are on the pages of a magazine, a television screen, a movie screen, or, very often, a computer screen—the end result is a polluted mind and a heart full of adultery. The lustful images take root in the individual and may never go away outside of a divine renovation of the heart and mind.

One lady I talked to said that she was misled to believe that if she watched pornography it would stimulate her to being more amorous toward her husband. So she rented a video. What she thought would help her be more receptive to her husband actually became the sexual images she saw when she was with him sexually. She said that video remained in her mind for decades. To her horror she could see those images anytime she let her mind think about that one-time mistake. She has confessed and asked God to forgive her sin of ignorance and disobedience.

Why is it so difficult to get sexual images out of our minds? Neil Anderson said in his wonderful book *Finding Freedom in a Sex-Obsessed World*, "When we are stimulated emotionally—which includes being visually stimulated by sexual images—a signal is sent to our glands. A hormone called epinephrine is secreted into the bloodstream, which locks into our memory whatever stimulus is present at the time of the emotional excitement. This reaction causes us to involuntarily remember emotionally charged events—negative and traumatic ones as well as positive ones."[2] He goes on to say, "It has been said that three viewings of hard-core pornography have the same lasting effect on us as actual sexual experience."

Often we think that pornography is only a man's problem. We assume that only men get caught in the trap of sexual addictions. But that is not the case. "Satan goes about like a roaring lion, seeking someone to devour." The gender of the victim is a nonissue. Women are just as capable of playing fools as men. We should all be on guard to keep a watch over our eyes, hearts, and minds. Sin cannot be contained. Years ago I heard someone say, "Sin takes us further than we intended to stray, keeps us longer than we ever intended to stay, and exacts a heavier price than we ever intended to pay." The sin of pornography can definitely fuel this dreadful progression.

The effects of premarital physical involvement, pornography, and other hindrances to restoring and keeping purity in the marriage union can be overcome by God's redemptive grace. Along with the work that He is allowed to do in our lives, there are some things we can do that will contribute to the health of the oneness that couples long for.

Recapture Time and Desire

Using questionnaires completed by women all across the country has been most useful in researching what women are thinking about and dealing with. One question I have included more recently is: "What is the biggest challenge you and your spouse face as it pertains to your sexual relationship?" These are the two most common responses:

- We don't have enough time for one another
- I have lost my desire for sex

If a lack of time and desire are the most pressing issues, more attention and effort are necessary in these areas to make your sexual relationship what God intended it to be. And what is God's plan for the marital union? Exhilaration and satisfaction!

Fast Food or Fine Dining?

Even the most careful health-nuts have times when they are caught unprepared and end up eating fast food. I know there have been times when I've been out shopping and have been ravenously hungry but didn't have time to sit down and eat something well prepared or nutritious. What was the solution? I'd stop and grab something quick. Eating fast food on occasion can be justified.

It fills a need; hunger is satisfied. However, we should never confuse "grabbing a bite" with having a meal. We know that we will become unhealthy, bloated, and even sick if the occasional junk food becomes our regular diet.

Now, think of the sexual relationship with your spouse as feeding an appetite, which it is. In the same way that a steady diet of fast food can be detrimental to our physical health, feeding our sexual appetites with a fast-food mentality can be just as harmful. Admittedly, when a couple is constantly stressed with time pressures and misplaced priorities it is easy to fall into the "grab a quickie" routine.

To carry this food/appetite metaphor a little further, consider the following comparison. If hurried sex is "fast food," "fine dining" is true intimacy with our spouses. Yes, a fast-food type of sex might satisfy physical hunger, but we should not forget that true intimacy satisfies the appetite for the deeper soul hunger connection that a husband and wife experience.

Think carefully about the deliberate preparations required to enjoy a night of fine dining:

- Reservations made ahead of time.

- Each one should take a bath and get dressed for the occasion.

- There needs to be provisions for someone to take care of the children.

- There is anticipation about the evening. It is more than just a meal; it is an event.

- Fine dining takes time. We eat in courses. There is no rush to finish eating and get out of the restaurant.

- The emphasis is on the quality of the dining, not the quantity of the serving.

- We don't eat out like this every evening. It is a special meal.

- We talk about what a wonderful time we had and look forward to going back.

Yes, fine dining is different than just eating a fast-food meal. The expense involved is noticeably more. For example, it will cost you time (plan ahead), and it will cost you money (hiring a babysitter, perhaps going to a local hotel for the evening to get away from the demands at home). Even though fine dining is more involved than just "grabbing something to eat," the results are a healthy, satisfying, rewarding experience.

An Uncommon Oneness

The goal of our sexual time together with our spouses is not to achieve orgasm, although that may occur. The goal of intimacy is to enjoy a level of oneness that is uncommon. It is not only about getting what we need, but about giving to our spouses what they need. You can say, "It is not about me; it is about us."

The weather conditions in the bedroom depend on how stormy the rest of the house may be. Men are able to compartmentalize their feelings, and this has been a source of frustration for women probably since the beginning of time. I talked to one frazzled lady who said, "It amazes me that my husband and I can have a horrible fight—there are verbal salvos launched and emotional shrapnel can litter the house. But when 11 o'clock comes around, he's on me like a chicken on a June bug. How does he do it? How can he be mean and hateful to me one minute and then want intimacy the next?"

The answer is simple. Her husband is functioning out of *eros* and not *agape* love. I realize my statement may offend the husband, and he might react with, "You don't even know me. How can you say I'm not loving my wife with God's kind of love?" He would be right. I don't know him, but I do recognize *agape* love when I see it. And the love that his wife described is no where near the kind, patient, selfless, giving love described in 1 Corinthians 13.

But are men the only ones capable of being thoughtless and selfish? No. Women are just as likely to function outside of *agape* love as men. I know friends who have admitted to using sex as a weapon to punish or manipulate to get their way.

The marital relationship between a husband and wife is to be a wonderful experience for both. As wives, we are privileged to serve our husbands in the area of their sexual needs. Ladies, let me remind you of what God has to say about the sexual union between a married couple:

> Drink water from your own cistern, and fresh water from your own well. Should your springs be dispersed abroad, streams of water in the streets? Let them be yours alone, and not for strangers with you. Let your fountain be blessed, and rejoice in the wife [or husband] of your youth. As a loving hind and a graceful doe, let her breast satisfy you at all times. Be exhilarated always with her love (Proverbs 5:15-19).

I'll close this chapter with a wonderful, lyrical look at a marriage that hasn't lost its pizzazz! Maybe you experience this regularly. I hope so!

We Get in Trouble When We Kiss

We get in trouble when we kiss
We get in trouble when we kiss like this
There ought to be a law against our lips
We get in trouble when we kiss

We were both late for work again this morning
We almost left on time; you know we tried
I almost lost my job; you got a warning
Guess we ought to shake hands when we say goodbye

'Cause we get in trouble when we kiss
We get in trouble when we kiss like this
There ought to be a law against our lips
We get in trouble when we kiss

I flew in; you met me at the curb
I climbed inside the car; we kissed hello
That whistle was the next thing that we heard
And Barney Fife was screaming, "You're holding up the show."

'Cause we get in trouble when we kiss
We get in trouble when we kiss like this
There ought to be a law against our lips
We get in trouble when we kiss

My Uncle Jack got sick, and then he died
We were sitting in the service that they had
Everything was going alright
Until you just had to kiss me 'cause I was looking sad
Oh!

We get in trouble when we kiss
We get in trouble when we kiss like this
There ought to be a law against our lips
We get in trouble when we kiss[3]

4

I Want My Husband to Know

I Will Do My Part to Create
a Safe and Secure Home

LATE ONE NIGHT STEVE AND I were driving back to our home in Tennessee from one of our weekend engagements. We started the trip late in the evening. We knew it would be a long night, but it didn't matter. We just wanted to get home. When we started our journey the weather was fine, but the longer we drove the worse it got. Before long large drops of rain began to splatter on the windshield. In just a few moments those raindrops turned into large buckets of water splashing our windshield, blinding us, making it hard to see on-coming traffic.

With each passing 18-wheeler our visibility became more and more nonexistent. Although we had slowed our van to a crawl with the hazard lights blinking out a warning to all approaching vehicles, the rest of the world seemed to think it was Sunday afternoon at the Charlotte Speedway. Cars zoomed past us, seemingly unaware that one wrong turn of the wheel, one flooded dip in the highway, would send us all into a junkyard of tangled metal and broken bodies.

Although I wasn't the one in control of the steering wheel, I drove every inch of the trip. With white knuckles gripped around the armrest, my feet firmly planted on the floor, and my eyes wide as saucers, I kept my optical radar scanning the highway, waiting for the moment of impact. The muscles in the back of my neck ached as each mile snail-crawled by. Finally after what seemed like an eternity of toe-curling tension and waterfall rain, I saw it. Our exit. Nothing could have been a more welcomed sight. As we made the gradual turn off the interstate and on to exit 24, we continued slowly to the right. The next sight I longed to see was the white vinyl faux fence entrance into our driveway.

As our van came to a stop beside the garage, all the stress and strain of the past six hours melted away. A hot bath and a soft, warm bed would take care of the rest of my muscle aches. As I finally laid my head on the soft pillow on our cozy bed, safely spooned against my husband's back, I drifted off to sleep. The howling wind and torrential rain that had moments before sent a shiver up my spine and terror into my heart became a lullaby that rocked me to sleep. I was finally home, and we were safe and sound.

Home is supposed to be that kind of safe harbor for a family. Regardless of the weather conditions outside, home is to be that soft, warm place where the rest of the world is kept at bay.

When our son, Nathan, was in junior high school he came home one day describing what his day had been like. He told of being teased and tormented by the resident bully of the school. He told us how beat up and disrespected he felt. And then he said something I will never forget: "Mom, no matter how bad it gets out there, no matter what they do to me, I know if I can get through the front door of our home I'm safe."

There's nothing quite like the feeling of a "safe house." We all need a sanctuary where we know we're not only out of harm's way, but we're also unconditionally loved and accepted. And a spouse who might spend a day out in the world taking the punches of the "job bully" especially needs the sheltering comfort of a home to return to.

After Nathan married, he wrote a song for his wonderful wife, Stephanie. Contained within the lyrics of this song is the youthful determination to make home a safe place. Steve and I have also adopted the sentiments in this song.

Weather It All

I know in the summer, love grows
And in the winter, time slows
We'll weather it all
I'll build a fire and hold you close
We'll weather it all
Bring you a red, red rose.

I know on the sea, ships toss and turn
And in the fire, chaff burns
We'll weather it all
Our love's made of gold
We'll weather it all
Our sail will not fold.

Driving down the back roads, Tennessee
Some live in fortune, some in poverty
We'll weather it all
These times will not last
We'll weather it all
Riches gone or hard times past.[1]

In the Song of Solomon we read,

> Put me like a seal over your heart, like a seal on your
> arm. For love is as strong as death, jealousy is as severe as
> Sheol; its flashes are flashes of fire, the very flame of the
> LORD. Many waters cannot quench love, nor will rivers
> overflow it; if a man were to give all the riches of his
> house for love, it would be utterly despised (8:6-7).

The Message Bible puts it this way:

> Hang my locket around your neck, wear my ring on
> your finger. Love is invincible facing danger and death.
> Passion laughs at the terrors of hell. The fire of love stops
> at nothing—it sweeps everything before it. Flood waters

can't drown love, torrents of rain can't put it out. Love
can't be bought, love can't be sold—it's not to be found
in the marketplace.

Wow! That's beautiful.

It is undeniable that troubles will come. You know this is true.
But if you had any doubt, John 16:33 will take it away. God promises
His children, "In the world you have tribulation." As disconcerting
as that verse sounds, I'm so glad Jesus didn't stop with that sobering
warning. He went on to say, "But take courage; I have overcome the
world." Jesus has promised us that He is bigger than any trouble,
stronger than any storm that might blow our way and threaten to
topple us.

The Tornadoes of Trouble

To overcome the problems of life and maintain the safe harbor
of home, we need to heed the warning signs and prepare for what
might come our way. In our region of the country, a tornado is a
common intruder. One of the deadliest characteristics of a twister
is how it can surprise humans with its presence.

Kim is one of my dearest friends. She and I met when we were
both speaking at a ladies' conference in her home state of Florida.
She now lives in the Nashville area not too far from me. One day
Kim was telling me about the damage that had been done to her
parents' home in Florida after a series of hurricanes. She said, "I grew
up in Florida, and hurricanes were something you just learned to
live with. I was never really scared of them because we knew when
they were coming. The weather man usually gave us plenty of time
to prepare for them. Actually, you know a hurricane is coming days
in advance." She went on to say, "However, I've never gotten used
to living in Tennessee. Here we don't have hurricanes, we have tornadoes. While hurricanes typically give us fair warning, tornadoes
can just pop up. In Tennessee you can go to bed and everything is
all right. However, you might wake up in the middle of the night
to find that your roof has been ripped off, and, worse, you've been

picked up and landed in a swamp down the road." She said, "I'll take a hurricane over a tornado any day. I'd rather be able to prepare for the storm that's coming."

I agree with Kim. The worst kinds of storms are the ones that catch us off guard. Let's look at some of the storms a couple might face.

When the Twister Is a Wayward Child

Bill and Debbie raised their children in church. There was no question that Christ was the center of their lives and the Lord of their home. Both parents were involved in their kids' school activities. They were in attendance for every ball game, every music recital.

By the time they spotted the emotional tornado cutting a path straight through the heart of their home, the damage was already done. Their oldest son was in trouble. Suddenly the parents were using terms they never thought they would ever use in connection with one of their precious children: drug rehab, porno websites, probation, college drop-out. It seemed too much to endure. Like any tornado, this trouble seemed to pop up overnight, but the damage wasn't as quickly swept away.

No doubt about it, the safe harbor this home had once enjoyed was now being pummeled by the flying debris of anger, disappointment, grief, blame, and regret. Even though everyone who knew this couple tried to comfort them and tell them they had done a good job as parents, Bill and Debbie still internalized the heartbreak of having a child who had chosen the wrong path.

Where does a parent go for help when a child is in trouble? When children are younger there are more manageable things that can be done. You can take away simple privileges, such as toys and TV shows. You can make life miserable enough that they will want to do the right thing. But when a child is grown and out of the parents' sight and influence, for the most part there is only one place to go: straight into the arms of the Savior.

My mother- and father-in-law understand the threat of this tornado. When Steve was in his late teens and entering into his early twenties, he took his parents on a sad journey. After he left home he joined the Navy. It was there that he had opportunities to do things he didn't have access to when he was safe in the home of his godly parents. However, his folks didn't despair. They did what they had done all their Christian lives when the devil tried to destroy the safe harbor of their home. They called on the only one who can unscramble eggs, the one who makes good out of bad situations. They were limited in what they could do physically, but they believed in the unlimited ability of the one who could reach their son, whom some considered unreachable. As a result, prodigal Steve eventually came home to Christ.

While there are many examples of tornadoes that can tear through a home, there is nearly none that can rival the trauma of a wayward child. If this is the storm that has troubled your life, find comfort in the words of Psalm 27:13: "I would have despaired unless I had believed that I would see the goodness of the Lord in the land of the living. Wait for the Lord; be strong and let your heart take courage; yes, wait for the Lord." May you also find solace in the song that Steve wrote to honor his parents and their devotion to prayer on his behalf.

Reachable

There's a boy in his mother's prayers
'Cause lately she's been aware
That he's been drifting too far from the shore
And she's beginning to believe
The boy is getting out of reach
Weary mother, don't you worry anymore.

'Cause the boy is reachable, I know he's reachable
And to God he's visible, and all things are possible
'Cause if the Lord can reach his hand of love through time
And touch a cold sinner's heart like mine
The boy is reachable, oh, yes, he's reachable

There's a girl on her daddy's heart
'Cause lately they've drifted apart
And the company she's keeping leads her further away
And he's beginning to believe the girl is getting out of reach
Weary father, don't you worry anymore

The girl is reachable, I know she's reachable
And to God she's visible, and all things are possible
'Cause if the Lord can reach his hand of love through time
And touch a cold sinner's heart like mine
The girl is reachable, oh, yes, she's reachable[2]

The Hurricane of Infidelity

There are tornadoes that catch us unaware. But, as my friend Kim said, there are storms we can see coming, even some we knowingly bring on ourselves. Of all that could be mentioned, one of the most important ones that should be addressed is infidelity. The reason I put it at the top of the list is because it is one of those storms that cannot only be predicted but also is one that can be avoided. Throughout the Scriptures we are warned about the sin of adultery. In Proverbs 6:27-29 it says, "Can a man take fire in his bosom and his clothes not be burned? Or can a man walk on hot coals and his feet not be scorched? So is the one who goes in to his neighbor's wife; whoever touches her will not go unpunished."

If you live anywhere in the world that is prone to hurricanes, there are things you can and should do to protect your house. In the same way, any of us who live and breathe and are married live in a potential danger zone that must be protected from the devastation of unfaithfulness.

God has given us a straightforward warning in Proverbs 7. Even though the passage features a man being seduced by a woman, we should all take these words as a warning. The ability to be led astray, enticed, and spiritually assaulted is not a gender issue. Both women and men are equally capable of playing fools. Let these words from

The Message serve as a weather report that a hurricane is blowing
in. It's time to batten down the hatches.

Dear Friend, do what I tell you;
treasure my careful instructions.
Do what I say and you'll live well
My teaching is as precious as your eyesight—guard it!
Write it out on the back of your hands;
etch it on the chambers of your heart.
Talk to Wisdom as to a sister.
Treat Insight as your companion.
They'll be with you to fend off the Temptress—
that smooth-talking, honey-tongued Seductress.

As I stood at the window of my house
looking out through the shutters,
watching the mindless crowd stroll by,
I spotted a young man without any sense
Arriving at the corner of the street where she lived,
then turning up the path to her house.
It was dusk, the evening coming on,
the darkness thickening into night.
Just then, a woman met him—
she'd been lying in wait for him, dressed to seduce him.
Brazen and brash she was,
restless and roaming, never at home,
Walking the streets, loitering in the mall,
hanging out at every corner in town.

She threw her arms around him and kissed him,
boldly took his arm and said,
"I've got all the makings for a feast—
today I made my offerings, my vows are all paid,
So now I've come to find you,
hoping to catch sight of your face—and here you are!
I've spread fresh, clean sheets on my bed,

colorful imported linens.
My bed is aromatic with spices
and exotic fragrances.
Come, let's make love all night,
spend the night in ecstatic lovemaking!
My husband's not home; he's away on business,
and he won't be back for a month."

Soon she has him eating out of her hand,
bewitched by her honeyed speech.
Before you know it, he's trotting behind her,
Like a calf led to the butcher shop,
like a stag lured into ambush
and then shot with an arrow,
Like a bird flying into a net
not knowing that its flying life is over.

So, friends, listen to me,
take these words of mine most seriously.
Don't fool around with a woman like that;
don't even stroll through her neighborhood.
Countless victims come under her spell;
she's the death of many a poor man.
She runs a halfway house to hell,
fits you out with a shroud and a coffin.

PROVERBS 7

How to Be Your Husband's Lover

Proverbs 7 contains plenty of instruction to help any observant wife recognize the oncoming storm that a seductress can bring into a marriage. Have you ever considered the fact that the methods she uses to lure a man can be used by a wife to capture her husband's attention? After all, the temptress must have had a good understanding of what it took to appeal to a man's desires. For that reason, I propose that we examine her techniques and determine if they are redeemable and can be creatively utilized. Ultimately, the goal is to keep your husband's eyes turned toward home, to make home a safer place by warding off the hurricane of adultery.

Following the chronology of Proverbs 7, the first thing the seductress did was use her knowledge of the man.

The key to the other woman's appeal to the man is not in how she makes him feel about her. It's all about how she makes him feel about himself. A man will not always leave his wife and family for a woman who is prettier, younger, thinner, smarter, or nicer. Very often a man will throw away everything precious to him for a woman who makes him feel desirable, virile, strong, youthful, and important. Oh, I hope you can hear this truth before the howl of a storm comes. Listen, my sisters! Be wise as serpents and innocent as doves. Look and learn from the Proverbs 7 woman.

She dressed for the occasion. She made herself alluring.

Being attractive is not about having the body of a supermodel. Your husband doesn't expect you to be a size 2 or have a surgically enhanced, perfect body. Making ourselves attractive is simply being our very best. A few years ago I heard someone say, "She's just as cute as she can be." I believe that's what we're talking about here. It's not being as "cute" as your sister or about being as beautiful as you were when you were 20. It's not about trying to live up to Hollywood's idea of lovely or being as adorable as the pastor's wife. It's about being as cute as *you* can be.

It's a dead-end street to compare ourselves with women on magazine covers that have been airbrushed and perfected by high-tech computer programs. Our efforts should be to look the best we can look and forget about everyone else.

Often women get miffed and allow their feelings to be hurt if their husbands indicate that they would like them to make some kind of change in their appearance. Perhaps the husband wants his wife to pay more attention to her diet, or maybe he wants her to start working out at the gym, or start taking a walk in the evenings.

Even though initially we wives might take offense at the suggestion that we need to work on our appearance, we should humble ourselves and prayerfully consider the suggestion for the sake of our marriages. As much as we might resent the fact, men are visual and they appreciate beauty.

Women sometimes assume because the husband is commanded by God to unconditionally love his wife like Christ loves His church, that the husband has no right to *expect* his wife to always present herself in a lovely manner. Husbands are to represent Jesus to us and, therefore, the husband is to accept his wife warts, flannel gown, 20-year-old bedroom slippers, and all. Ladies, let me remind you that when Jesus comes back for His bride, He is looking for a lover who is fit, beautiful, and dressed for the occasion.

In Ephesians 5:25-27 it says, "Husbands, love your wives, just as Christ also loved the church and gave Himself up for her, so that He might sanctify her, having cleansed her by the washing of water with the word, that He might present to Himself the church in all her glory, having no spot or wrinkle or any such thing; but that she would be holy and blameless." While this passage implies that Christ, the groom, desires to cleanse His bride, His work with her includes her cooperation. A wife should make the effort to look as good as she can. Why would we not give the same effort to keeping our men as the wicked harlot would make to stealing them? And by all means, a wife should resist the temptation to assume that it is her husband's duty to love her no matter how she let's herself go and how sloppy she looks when he comes home. Living under that kind of assumption is the recipe for heartache. That attitude is not being a wise woman.

She seizes him with kisses. She is affectionate.

Were you more affectionate with your husband when you were first married than you are now? If you have slacked off in the area of physical affection, remember how important it is. God created us as physical beings. For instance, do you give your husband freshly brushed hair and brushed teeth along with a good morning kiss as he goes off to work? If you have been too tired to get up and freshen up, today is the day to start. Set your alarm for 15 minutes earlier than usual, get up, attend to your hygiene, and before he goes off to work give him something to think about during the day.

In the previous chapter we discussed making ourselves sexually available to our spouses. Don't underestimate the importance of the sexual relationship to a man. When he knows his wife loves him and wants to be with him sexually, there is nearly nothing he won't do for her. The harlot makes sure the man feels loved and cared for when it comes to giving affection. Should we do any less for the men God has given to us?

She spreads her bedroom with beautiful coverings.
She is prepared.

Notice the seductress didn't save her best linens for company. No, she thought the man was important enough to bring out the best. Let me encourage you—if there is only enough budget to remodel or update one room in the house, let it be your bedroom. Pick a color you both love. Make the room special.

Not only should we make our bedroom beautiful, but we should make it different than any other room in the house.

Eliminate Clutter

Take a look at your bedroom. Is it cluttered with magazines and clothes hanging over the chair? Can you write your name in the dust that covers the dresser? Don't invite your husband into a nasty, dirty bedroom. When you see clutter and mess, clean it up. Either throw it away, give it away, or find a place to put it out of your sight. When a bedroom is piled with unnecessary stuff, it loses its "loving room" appeal.

Eliminate Other Uses for the Room

I understand you may be cramped for space, but try to eliminate other uses for your bedroom. For instance, if you presently use one corner of your bedroom for a home office, consider making a change. Even if you have to give up a dining room or part of the den, if at all possible try to keep the bedroom special. Having a constant reminder of unfinished work or an unpleasant project in the bedroom can distract from the purpose of the bedroom being a haven, a place where the world is far away.

Eliminate the TV

I know I've just lost some of you at this point. Television is an intricate part of the average American family's life. But why does it have to be included in the most sacred room of the house? Often when couples complain about their relationships, they cite the lack of meaningful time together. Yet those same couples will spend precious time with Letterman and Leno every evening. If you want to watch television, go into the den and watch it. If you want intimate time with your spouse, reserve the bedroom for that special purpose. Keep that sacred promise of not allowing others into the bed with you.

Eliminate Conflict from the Bedroom

Keeping the bedroom sacred also entails keeping conflicts out of the bedchamber. If you begin discussing an issue and feel the conversation taking a confrontational turn, get up and go into another room and work it out. If you argue, do it in any room in the house except the bedroom. The bedroom should be reserved for pleasant and private conversation.

She prepared the bedroom with wonderful aromas.
The love-chamber exuded sensual love and sexual satisfaction.

There are many ways we can set an enticing mood in our bedrooms. We can light some candles. Not only are scented candles a subtle mood enhancer, but I dare to guess that most of us look better in candlelight than in the unforgiving glare of an iridescent light bulb. Make use of soft, lovely music. I think it's best to use music that doesn't include words. You want your husband to be thinking about you, not singing along with his favorite song.

If your husband likes perfume, use a dab on your neck and between your breasts. Human beings are excited by smell. Keep in mind that a successfully romantic evening with your spouse may or may not involve sexual intimacy. Connecting with a spouse needs to be whatever the two of you need it to be. What each of you needs most may simply be an evening of talking with one another, spending time with one another. The idea is to enjoy oneness.

She initiates the sexual encounter. Her words were alluring and provocative.

Husbands need to know their wives want them sexually. A woman who gives sex but is emotionally uninvolved is disrespecting and embarrassing her husband. It brings shame to him when he feels undesirable to his wife. If the wife has lost her sexual desire due to hormonal changes in her life or is suffering from postpartum fluctuations in her body, she should find a friend or a counselor who understands her situation. Getting good advice about what to do in this area is wise.

I strongly urge you not to tell your husband you have lost your sexual desire for him. This is one subject, in my opinion, that should not be discussed with your spouse. If you tell him, long after you have remedied your libido problem, he will remember your lack of desire for him. Some men are not as tough and resilient as we may have been led to believe. No man wants to think his spouse is repelled by him, even if it is not his fault. So, ladies, be wise, keep quiet, and seek help from others who can assist you.

She uses words that are persuasive. She entices him.

The tongue is one of the most persuasive tools we have in our toolbox. Use your words to build up your man. "Pleasant words are a honeycomb, sweet to the soul and healing to the bones" says Proverbs 16:24. Nothing is quite as powerful as our verbal communication with our spouses. Of course we must realize that what we are really saying is a whole lot more than the actual words we use. Are you wise at heart? Proverbs 16:23 says that if you are wise you will teach your mouth to be sweet and persuasive. Isn't it comforting to know that controlling our tongue is something we can learn? Take the time to examine your communication. Listen to the words that are coming out of your mouth. Take note of the tone with which they are delivered. Consider your body language. I once heard that 55 percent of all communication is nonverbal. And 38 percent of what we say is reflected in the tone of our voice. Only 7 percent is the actual words we use. Considering that communication involves the whole person, what messages are you sending to your spouse? Does he hear honor and respect in the words, tone, and attitude you use with him? Or does he feel like a child who is being corrected and belittled by an angry parent? Are your words argumentative? Do you manipulate to get your own way? Do you pout or complain when something isn't as you think it should be?

The words we communicate to one another as husband and wife will either set the mood for loving or for loathing. We can't castrate our men with our tongues and then expect them to respond to us in the loving manner we desire. As women of God, our words should be used not for our advantage but for the building up of our mates.

She builds him with words that make him feel good about himself.

People need affirming words of encouragement. Even men who shun a compliment or act like they don't want to hear how great you think they are still need to hear it. At least once a week I tell Steve something along the lines of "No one in the world is as loved and cherished as you are. You are the best! You are the smartest. You are the nicest and the most talented. You are the best-looking man in the whole world." You might say, "Isn't it wrong to flatter a person?

Won't it make him conceited?" Let me tell you, ladies. The world is constantly tearing our men down. So many of them get beat up, used up, passed over, and ripped off on a regular basis. We need to be on their sides. If our words are grounded in our feelings for our man, it's not flattery—it's the truth!

A husband who is confident that his wife is on his side and thinks that he's wonderful will walk with a spring in his step and his shoulders pulled back. When a man knows he is doing a good job at home, he will face his work and the world with more confidence. Conversely, a man who is a gigantic success at work and a big man in other people's eyes will inwardly feel like a failure if he is unable to keep the woman he loves satisfied and fulfilled. Our assurance to him that he is doing a good job at home will mean more to him than any promotion or advancement he could earn at work.

As I encourage Steve with my words, guess what he does? He reciprocates kind, affirming words.

Bring New Life to Your Marriage

The end result of what the harlot did to the young, naive man in Proverbs 7 led him to the grave. His doom is sealed. However, with a redemptive approach to drawing in our husbands, we may be able to bring new life to our marriages.

Am I guaranteeing that if we glean from the methods of the Proverbs 7 woman and become more sexually accessible and more positive toward our husbands they will never stray? No, I'm not trying to do that. However, I am saying that if we are mindful of their needs and meet them joyfully, then the responsibility for any bad decision our husbands might make in the area of moral fidelity is their own. Each one of us is responsible to possess our own vessel in sanctification and honor (1 Thessalonians 4:4). Ultimately, it is not our responsibility if our spouses choose to stray. And, conversely, it's not their fault if we choose the path of the fool. One of our jobs as husbands and wives is to make being faithful as easy as possible. Let this lyric encourage you to tell your man how much he means to you.

Easy to Steal

His wife is beautiful
She has a face to die for
Why he walked out her door
Who knows?

And the woman he's with now
Everybody's sayin', "She's a step down"
But she won his heart somehow
And it shows

Then I heard it from a good friend
What she did to get to him
She didn't touch him with her hands
She just whispered in his ear

I guess it's true, it's not just how she looks
It's how she makes him feel
And she knew if she used the right words
She could turn his wheel
The truth of the matter
The man who can be flattered
Is easy to steal, easy to steal

She told him he was a good man
She told him she was his biggest fan
It wasn't new, but it was something
He needed to hear
The truth of the matter
The man who can be flattered
Is easy to steal.[3]

It is also wise to help each other rise to the high standard of faith-fulness. One method we heard of that a couple used to upgrade the trust factor in their marriage, thus making it a safer place for them both to live, merits being passed along. Steve reveals their very note-worthy accountability method in the following lyric.

Faithful to You

Thirty years ago, one night in May
He came home from work in a strangely quiet way
Just before they closed their eyes and drifted off to rest
He turned to her and whispered, "I must confess."

"Well, you know a salesman's life is a lot of time alone
Today, I made a call, 'bout sixty miles from home
And there was a woman with a look in her eyes
And the thought that crossed my mind took me by surprise."

"But I can end this day with peace in my heart
Though I was away, and we were miles apart
I can come back home and tell you it is true
Today, I've been faithful, faithful to you."

So that night they made a promise
And bathed it in their tears
That all their days would end like this
They've kept it through the years
And it's helped them in those moments
When love was put to test
To know that night they'd face each other
And from their hearts confess.

"I can end this day with peace in my heart
Though I was away, and we were miles apart
I can come back home and tell you it is true
Today, I've been faithful, faithful today.
And by the Savior's grace, I can tell you it is true
I'll always be faithful, faithful to you."[4]

Everyone wants and needs a safe harbor in the midst of the storms of life. God has designed that our homes be that place of safety. I want my husband to know that I am willing, even longing, to work together with him to create a place built on the firm foundation of Christ, who alone can help us withstand any storm that comes our way.

5

I Want My Husband to Know

I Admire the Way He Provides for Our Family

I WANT MY HUSBAND TO know I will do whatever I can to help lighten the load he carries when it comes to our finances.

Recently Steve and I attended a wedding. The bride and groom were the children of some friends from two states away. No doubt about it, the parents of the bride sure knew how to put on a show. No expense was spared in making this a memorable day for everyone in attendance. The church where the service was held was meticulously decorated with beautifully arranged flower displays. The music that graced the event was carefully selected and magnificently executed. And, of course, the bride and groom could not have been more adorable.

The handsome groom stood at the front of the church awaiting the arrival of his beloved. Clothed in his elegant, ever-so-expensive tuxedo he looked the completed picture of enviable masculinity. As he majestically posed, the music started and all eyes turned expectantly to the back of the church for the entrance of the bride. She began her graceful glide down the aisle flawlessly displaying the designer gown made especially for her.

As the ceremony began, the bride and groom looked deep into each other's eyes. Everyone in the room could sense they were filled with the expectations of total and utter marital happiness. All those who loved them and loved their families were sending positive thoughts their way. Yes, others might fail to keep marital promises, but we were confident they were going to make it.

All I could do was pray that the emotionally packed euphoria that ran up and down their spines as they held each other's hands were feelings based on more than just a strong physical chemistry and a soul mate compatibility.

Those of us in attendance sat and listened to the young lovers make their forever promises. They pledged to stay together regardless of what unforeseen storms might blow through their lives.

"In sickness and in health."

Even though they both stood there shining with the healthy glow of youthful vitality, they promised that even when the petals have fallen from their bloom and they are old, gray, lumpy, and stooped, they will still stay together and take care of one another.

"Forsaking all others."

They promised exclusivity. No other person would encroach into their lives. No one on the earth would ever hold the place of honor and preeminence that belonged to their spouse.

As I listened to this vow I had to chuckle to myself. I knew for a fact that the young bride still had her mother on "speed dial" and the young groom had insisted on continuing his traditional "boys night out" with his old college buddies.

And then they arrived at part of the list of promises that I knew could challenge them far more than they could ever imagine.

"For richer or for poorer."

When they made this promise, I knew they didn't have a clue about what they had just vowed. The engagement ring had payments attached that the man would be making for months, maybe years down the road. Their car was not their own but the property of a nearby bank. The apartment they were planning to occupy was not what newlyweds normally garner. It had more features than their parents' homes, including a hefty monthly payment to dwell there. Yet the couple looked at each other with straight faces and promised that money would never be an issue that would separate them. No doubt about it, this young husband and wife had a lot to learn in the coming days, months, years, and, hopefully, decades of marriage.

Those of us in the pews who had been married for some time knew they didn't understand what they were doing. Nonetheless, it was easy to get caught up in the "happily ever after" feelings that accompany those moments and we smiled.

I left the wedding chapel praying that this couple would defy the odds and that the love they pledged just moments before really would last the test of time…and especially the monthly payments.

The Love Killer

No couple starts out their life together intentionally planning to be part of the 50-plus percentile statistics of divorced couples. Nevertheless, many well-meaning pairs end up hating one another instead of hanging on to one another. And what is the culprit that brings so many young couples to the divorce court? Money!

When Steve and I got married West Virginia laws required that we use a minister who was licensed in that state to officiate the service. So we chose Pastor Fred McCallister, a local preacher, who agreed to perform the ceremony—but only if we would go to his office and talk. He wanted to do some last-minute, premarital counseling with us. We complied with his request even though we couldn't imagine why we would need counseling. To appease the preacher, we showed up for our 30-minute counseling session.

Though it was a brief meeting, it was long on wisdom. Among the several bits of timeless advice Pastor Fred offered, one of the things he said during our time with him was, "If you're going to have trouble in your marriage, it will probably be in three or four areas. One of the most common is money."

The pastor didn't detect it, but we both chuckled inside when he warned us about the potential danger money could cause. We silently snickered because we hardly had two pennies to rub together.

We figured we had wasted our time with the preacher. Were we ever wrong! Reality was only months away.

At the end of our first year of marriage we calculated that we had grossed about $3,000. Our work in a Christian country-rock-bluegrass-folksy-blues-type trio didn't generate much money. We had plenty of styles, but not much stipend. After paying tithe and bills and trying desperately to save a little, there wasn't any left over for the "goodies" that hard work was supposed to yield. One of the items we longed for, or at least I did, was a washer and dryer set.

I remember thinking out loud one day to Steve, "We don't vacation in Maui, and we don't make payments on an expensive car, so surely we can invest in a washing machine and a dryer." I was tired of going to the laundromat. It would be much more convenient if I didn't have to make the extra effort of carrying our clothes to the local coin-fed "Swishy-Washateria." I had all the reasons to justify the purchase, but the money was missing. So we did what any red-blooded American would do when he lacked the green stuff. We went to the appliance store and asked to put our purchases on credit.

We picked out a top-of-the-line Maytag set. (If we're going to be in debt, why not go all the way!) I could hardly wait for the day to arrive when the store was scheduled to deliver the washer/dryer combo to our little duplex apartment. All day long I waited for the call to set up a time for delivery. Late that afternoon they called and said they would not be coming. We were turned down for credit.

Can you believe it? They told us we didn't have any money. Well! Tell us something we didn't already know. If we had the money, we wouldn't need the credit. I cried great big tears that day as I loaded up our 1950 mint-green Chevy and went to the laundromat once again.

Looking back over the many years and several washer/dryer sets later, I realize that what broke my heart—being refused a credit line—turned out to be the kindest thing any merchant has ever done for us. I wish that other young couples would be so blessed as to be denied the opportunity to be in debt up to their eyeballs.

Nowadays a person doesn't have to qualify for credit. The credit card companies give out their "enslavement cards" to anyone who will sign up. The Bible warns us in Proverbs 22:7 that "the rich rule over the poor, and the borrower becomes the lender's slave." We seem to have forgotten the truth. It is ridiculous how easy it is to get a credit card today—and so many do.

In our book *What Husbands and Wives Aren't Telling Each Other,* Steve and I refer to the chapter on money issues as "Making a Living or Making a Killing." Our parents' generation was content to make a living for their families. Often the man was the sole financial provider for his family. He could feel good about himself if his family had a home to live in, food on the table, and a family car.

Today people want to make a killing. They want to strike it rich through the lotteries or investments. Willing to work hard, they still want to reach the top quickly and easily. And so many of us go into debt so we can have perks now.

Unfortunately, many in our generation believe—and we've taught our children—that just any house will *not* do. We have to live in our "dream house." As evidence of this attitude, take note of what today's people typically call a first house: a "starter home." What that actually means is "this house will have to do until we can do better." What's wrong with the starter-home mentality? Very simply, it keeps a couple constantly looking for something more, something bigger, and something better. The pressure to "move up" in the world is constant. Our grandparents and parents had a different view. When they bought their first house, very often it became their last house. Their homes became known to most of us as "the home place." Many times couples from the older generation would buy a home, birth and raise their children there, and die in the same dwelling. There was not the expectation moving beyond comfort to luxury.

Recently a radio broadcast featured an illustration about just how materialistic things have gotten. The broadcaster cited interesting trends in the real-estate industry. According to him, some home buyers are now demanding that houses include multiple appliances. Homeowners want *two* dishwashers per kitchen. They are now asking for a washer/dryer set *on each floor* of the house. One refrigerator? Are you kidding? We need one in the kitchen and one in the garage.

As the size of the average family has decreased, the square footage of the average home has increased. The average dimension of a home in the 1950s was around 900 square feet. The typical size of a home in 2005 was approximately 2400 square feet. Another sign of the times is found in the family room...well, now it's a special place called a media room with theater seating. The average home today has a TV in nearly every room.

The kitchen has become a deserted place. Fewer and fewer families are eating together. I recently heard about one family who was on the verge of bankruptcy. One of the reasons for their economic trouble is that they were spending—hang on to your wallet—$19,000 a year to eat out. And when they did eat at home, they didn't use real dishes and cutlery. They bought plastic utensils so they didn't have to wash them.

Another area of the home that holds plenty of evidence of potential money woes is the driveway and garage. Many families now own at least one car per driving-age member. Families no longer "make do" with one or two vehicles.

With society and media promoting more and more amenities as proof of success, is it any wonder that we feel the crushing pressure of financial demands?

But let me tell you a little secret. It *is* possible to live within your means...and be content and grateful for what you have.

How Can You Help Your Husband Carry the Load as Provider?

Statistically, more and more women are working outside the home to contribute to the income of the family. In light of the lifestyle expectations the modern-day family has, it's not surprising that both husband and wife are needed to contribute to the coffers. There may be situations where the wife may want to work exclusively inside the home, especially if she has small children, but many believe they have little choice but to seek outside employment. Granted, with the cost of living soaring out of reach, in certain parts of the country it is very difficult for a family to survive on one income.

During those lean years of our early marriage, I did all I could to increase our income. I babysat for a lady down the street while she went to work. When our son was just a baby, I put him in his stroller and walked around the neighborhood selling Avon cosmetics. I was very frugal with what little money we did have. The thought of going to a store and spending $10 or $20 just for the fun of it was simply out of the question. Every penny was accounted for because every penny was needed.

As wives, God has called us to be helpers to our husbands. There are some things we can do that can assist them in carrying the heavy burden of providing for the family financially.

Do All You Can to Contribute

In the book of Proverbs, chapter 31, we read about the virtuous woman. She not only looked after the affairs of her home, but she was also very industrious in bringing in money for the support of her family. Proverbs 31:11-16 says,

> The heart of her husband trusts in her, and he will have no lack of gain. She does him good and not evil all the days of her life. She looks for wool and flax and works with her hands in delight. She is like merchant ships; she brings her food from afar. She rises also while it is still night and gives food to her household and portions to her maidens. She considers a field and buys it; from her earnings she plants a vineyard.

The Proverbs 31 woman, as she is affectionately referred to, sounds like someone who is very involved with the financial welfare of her family. Even though no job is more important than the one a wife does inside her home, she should always be looking for ways to help out with the family economy.

Before a husband and wife decide they both have to work 40-to-60-hour-a-week jobs, they should take a good, hard look at just what they are working for:

• Are you both wearing yourself out and getting nowhere?

• Are you sacrificing for things that lose their value as soon as you bring them home? Are you investing irreplaceable time for depreciating stuff?

• Have your wants and desires led you down a path to financial slavery?

• Are you content to make a living or are you doing everything you can to "make a killing"?

Couples should sit down together and evaluate what is important to the family. Is it really worth what it is costing emotionally, spiritually, and even financially for both to be employed? Are the children suffering neglect because of a "treadmill existence"? (We look like we're doing something. We're sweating, feeling exhausted, panting for breath, but when we get off we are in the same place we started. "Oh, I went five miles today." Really, where did you go? "Nowhere. But I got really tired.")

There's no question that someone has to take on the responsibility of financial provision for the family. Should it be the husband? The wife? Both? Does it really matter who?

In the insightful book *For Women Only,* Shaunti Feldhahn cites the results of a national survey she conducted for the writing of her book. She discovered that there are at least seven things every woman should know about her husband. One of the chapters addresses how a man feels about his work. Mrs. Feldhahn states that a man carries a tremendous burden for the financial well being of his family. Even though the wife may work and contribute to the income, the husband takes on the primary responsibility to provide for his household. Feldhahn goes on to say that there may be some who would argue that it makes no difference if the man is the bread earner or if he stays at home and his wife provides for the family. There may be situations where the husband is unable to work because of some infirmity, and the wife must take on that role, but as a general rule, men have an innate desire and feel a calling to provide for and take care of the family.[1]

In the book of Genesis, 3:17-19, we can see that work was always part of God's plan for mankind. He said to Adam

> Because you have listened to the voice of your wife, and have eaten from the tree about which I commanded you, saying, "You shall not eat from it"; cursed is the ground because of you; in toil you will eat of it all the days of your life. Both thorns and thistles it shall grow for you; and you will eat the plants of the field; by the sweat of your face you will eat bread, till you return to the ground, because from it you were taken; for you are dust, and to dust you shall return.

It is a biblical truth that since the fall, men have been destined to toil and labor until they breathe their last breath. With that imprint on their hearts, is it any wonder men often find their identity in their work? Work is a good thing. It is built into a man to work. Working in itself is not the curse. It's dealing with the thorns and thistles while he toils that makes work so painfully laborious. No, work is a pleasure and a blessing for a man. The curse just made his work more difficult.

By the way, when the woman was judged for her part in the fall, she was sentenced to experience multiplied pain during childbirth. Before the fall, giving birth was to be a much easier process. It's important to understand that children were not the curse any more than working was the curse. No, it's the added pain and sacrifice that birthing and raising children require that reminds us of the curse that was the result of sin.

Consider another aspect of the curse placed on the woman. Her desire to be with Adam was intensified. I don't believe her wanting a close relationship with her husband or wanting to spend time with him is the curse. The effect of the curse, it seems, is the conflict that results when he needs to work and she wants him at home.

When spouses start to feel neglected, instead of blaming each other each one needs to accept this dilemma as part of the curse brought about because of sin. Does all this mean that women don't toil? I don't think so. But a woman's primary labor is at home.

One day I was watching a daytime talk show where they were debating the pros and cons of women working inside and outside of the home. Heidi was about ten years old. She looked at me and asked, "Are you a stay-at-home mom?" I said, "No, Heidi, you're a take-along kid!" I have worked with my husband all our married life. However, our work together included taking our children with us as we traveled. Even though I have been officially employed, I've never felt the emotional responsibility of providing financially for our family.

Affirm His Work

Thank your husband for the sacrifices he makes to provide for the family. An important principle to remember is that even as you encourage your spouse as provider, you must let him know that you love spending time with him. Work and family life require a delicate balance.

Even though Steve and I travel together, much of our week is spent at home recording and doing the daily work of our business. Very often during this particular time, we are both involved in writing books. Steve works best at night when the phone is quiet and there are no interruptions. I work best in the mornings or in the afternoon. I am much too sleepy to get much done past six o'clock in the evening. As a result, we are usually on different work schedules. We can easily average being in bed together about four hours a night. Typically Steve comes to bed around one or two in the morning, and I get up around five.

I choose not to take Steve's absence from the bed as a personal insult. I see his schedule as one of the hazards of being self-employed.

However, when I do begin to feel neglected, I have a unique way of telling him. I take a bath, fix my hair, and put on full makeup and a nice outfit. Then I go to the bottom of the stairs and call up to his office. In a cheerful voice I facetiously say, "Steve, I'm going to town to find me a boyfriend."

He usually responds rather quickly.

"That's nice, Honey. What would you say about me being your boyfriend?"

"Sure! I'd love that."

"Can you give me 20 minutes?"

"That would fine. I'll be ready."

Then we go out and spend time together. I'm willing to tell him what I need, and he's smart enough to listen and respond to me.

Now understand that I don't ask for large blocks of his time every week. I know he has deadlines just like I do. But if we're not careful, we can get way too distracted with our work and neglect each other.

Of course, this cloth cuts both ways. There are times when Steve asks me to stop doing laundry and come into the sunroom and watch a movie with him. I've tried pretending like I'm watching it while I fold clothes. That doesn't work any more than if he takes his work with him on our days together. No, I need to show him the same consideration when he needs my attention. Sometimes he'll say, "Leave the dishes and go with me to Home Depot." You'd think that would not be a hard thing to do for someone who thinks Home Depot or Lowes is as romantic as a fancy restaurant, but sometimes it is. However, when I leave my work behind and just enjoy the moment, it always turns out to be a wonderful couple of hours that often includes a hot cup of McDonald's coffee and good conversation. For us that's a sizzling date!

Verbally affirming our husbands not only includes thanking them for working hard, but also telling them when we need them to take some couple time.

Adhere to a Budget and Cooperate in Controlling Expenditures

Not only can we help lift the heavy provider burden that is on our husbands with an understanding attitude and our words of encouragement, but we can lighten their load by keeping to a mutually agreed upon budget.

Of course, agreeing on a budget is sometimes easier in theory than in reality. Yet one young couple I know is proof that even though it is a formidable challenge, it can be accomplished. While their journey to financial freedom may take a while, the ideas the wife shared with me sounded right on and very practical. I think you'll find them helpful, too:

> To simplify the budgeting dilemma that plagued our marriage, we found it useful to divide our finances into three categories. We sat down together and took an honest look at our "have-to's," our "need-to's," and our "want-to's."
>
> The "have-to" category was pretty basic. It was money that was earmarked for set expenditures like the mortgage, the tithe to our church, and, since my husband is self-employed, taxes. In addition to these, we included our car payment, utility bills, food, bank loans, and other obligations that we had deliberately taken on. These were responsibilities we had to meet each month, so we gave this category "first pickin's" of our funds.
>
> The "need-to" category is a bit more flexible. We discussed items that pop up occasionally, the often unwelcome "surprise" expenditures. For example, funds for car maintenance, dental appointments, and replacing an appliance. Haircuts, birthday gifts, and such were also a part of the "need-to's" in our budget.
>
> A very important area of our finances that both my husband and I agreed upon was the need to prepare for retirement and to put aside a percentage each month in our savings account. Although we might not be able to give the same amount toward them each month, we

recognized the need to keep them a priority. So agreeing on this "need-to" part of the budget was fairly smooth going.

You might guess that the most serious discussions and negotiations came when we looked at the "want-to" category. This was when we really needed to call upon the Lord to help us be fair, honest, and adult with each other. We also realized this is the category where we most often make our biggest money mistakes.

After a close look at where our money was going, we found that we were spending a noticeable percentage of our income on entertainment (eating out, concerts, NASCAR tickets, movies, parties, music CDs, and the like), home decorating, purchasing unnecessary clothes, vacations, cable television, and Starbucks. These were expenses that we needed to curtail or in some cases, totally eliminate for the sake of the financial wholeness of the family.

Since we were both convinced of the need and the rightness of some financial discipline in our family, we have continued down this "tight" road. Make no mistake, we are constantly rethinking and revamping our budget, trying to make room for more of our "want-to's," but we find we are both happier with each other and with our financial future when we cooperate.

There are books available that can teach us how to put together a budget for the family. A budget is not just for people who have a hard time making ends meet. A budget is a tool to help you know where your money is going.

Money matters can get rather complicated. I once heard it said that arguments over money are never about money. There's always a deeper issue. Very often money is the topic, but the real issue may be covert control, latent anger, or even the unhealthy treatment of self-medicating emotional pain through excessive spending.

One friend of mine complains constantly that her husband is never at home. He works a minimum of 80 hours a week. To deal with her feelings of abandonment, she is constantly buying things. It's a vicious cycle. Because he is gone, she compensates with what she calls "shop therapy." He feels justified in working the long hours because he has to pay for all the stuff she just bought. She feels neglected and resentful because she is pulling "single-parenting" duty. Sadly, the end result is that she seems to have emotionally disconnected from the marriage. This detachment comes through in a very subtle way. She never cooks.

Since he doesn't make the effort to come home for dinner, she gets take-out. One meal can easily cost $50, and it is a sum that is spent nearly every night. The more he works, the more she spends. This unhealthy cycle has continued for years. He feels like an ATM machine, and she feels unloved and abandoned. He finds his identity and fulfillment in his job, and she fills the loneliness with things.

Is there any hope for this couple and others like them? Of course! The first step toward finding that hope is to start talking to one another. And in their conversing, they must get past what they consider a disagreement over money and get to the core issues. Once they deal with the real issues of their relationship, then they can start to work together on their mountain of indebtedness.

The Lie that Leads to Overspending

There may be other root sources for indebtedness than just thoughtless overspending. A family might be in financial trouble because of mounting medical expenses. One sweet family I know has a child with cystic fibrosis. They spend all the money they make and more trying to keep their child alive. As it happens sometimes in this country, they make too much money to qualify for financial assistance. However, they don't make enough to be able to comfortably pay for all that is needed to meet the medical needs. The very poor are taken care of, and the very rich take care of themselves, but working middle-class families are often left out in the cold.

Without an intervention from God, this family lives knowing

they will never be out of debt. That's just reality. And there is no other alternative for them but to continue doing what they have to do. They have accepted the fact that they will never be able to retire, and they will be working to pay off medical expenses until they die.

Other than a catastrophic situation like the cystic fibrosis parents, what could be another root cause of indebtedness? We might think we are in debt because we spend more money than we bring in. And that's never a good plan. But the ultimate problem regarding debt could be what we believe. In fact, money problems began in the garden of Eden. How could that be, you ask? What tricked Eve into the deception Satan managed was that she believed the lies he told her. If you are in debt, it may be because you have also unknowingly believed a lie.

In the garden, the first thing Satan did was cast doubt on God's word: "Indeed, has God said, 'You shall not eat from any tree of the garden?'" Eve answered, "From the fruit of the trees of the garden we may eat; but from the fruit of the tree which is in the middle of the garden, God has said, 'You shall not eat from it or touch it, or you will die.'"

Where did Eve get that last bit of her statement—the touch it part? She added to what God said. Then Satan contradicted God's word: "You surely will not die!" he said.

Satan went from casting doubt on God's word, to debating God's word, to questioning God's care for us: "For God knows that in the day you eat from it your eyes will be opened, and you will be like God, knowing good and evil." This implies God doesn't have our best interest in mind. (See Genesis 3.)

The enemy of our souls has us right where he wants us when he can get us to believe the lie that God is not good, the lie that God is withholding something positive from us.

Eve, believing the lie, saw that the food was good, she desired it, she took it, she ate it, and then she gave it to her husband. The end result was a breach between God and mankind. That chasm would not be truly bridged until Christ came and sacrificed His life on the cross. Jesus became the conduit that would restore the relationship between God and man once again. This is the progression:

> What we believe determines what we think.
>
> What we think determines how we feel.
>
> How we feel determines what we do.
>
> And what we do determines who we are.

To show how this works, consider the following issue. When I was in grade school my brother teased me and said I was heavy. You might think, "What's the big deal about that? Everyone is teased about something when he or she is a kid."

That's true. The problem was not in what my brother said. The trouble was I believed him. I thought I was fat. Looking back now, I realize I only weighed 110 pounds. I was probably ten pounds heavier than I should have been. But that didn't matter. As far as I was concerned, I was morbidly obese. For some reason, I was an easy target for that lie. I believed I was fat.

Because I *believed* I was fat, I began to *think* of myself as a very fat person. Those thoughts led me to *feel* disgusted about myself. Feeling unattractive, I neglected my appearance. I felt that there was no hope for me; there was nothing I could do. I was hideous. I remember the day in elementary school when how I felt about myself led me to act a certain way. At lunch time they were serving my favorite food. Feeling like it was already too late to ever try slimming down, I went back for spaghetti and meatballs three times. I *acted* on my belief that I couldn't change. I began to regularly overeat and used food to console myself. What was the result? I *became* a fat person. By the time I started college I was 80 pounds overweight. My weight wasn't really my problem; it was merely a symptom of my problem. I believed a lie.

Just as being overweight was the *result* rather than the root of my problem, believing a lie is at the heart of many of our money problems. It isn't pleasant when creditors start hounding us at home. It's a terrible feeling when we see the mail and wonder what little surprises are waiting for us in the stack of credit card notices. As unnerving as it is to be in debt to creditors, ultimately we must find "the lie" at the bottom of the money pit and remove it if we are to be free. The following illustrates a core money problem:

> We *believe* possessing things can make us happy.
> Our attention and allegiance go toward that pursuit.
>
> We *think* about those things that will make us happy.
> Thus we are never satisfied with what we have.
>
> We *feel* deprived when we don't get what we want.
> Since we don't have the money to buy them,
> *we charge* on credit cards.
>
> As a result of purchasing the things we believe will make us happy, even though we don't have the money, we *become* mired in debt.

Believing the lie that happiness is in what we possess, we end up owing more money than we can pay. Thus we are in debt. We can cut up our credit cards, consolidate our bills, get on a budget, and stick to it. However, until we deal with the lie that possessions will make us feel good about ourselves and make us happy, we will continue the debt/freedom cycle.

What is the antidote to the "lie" behind the debt dilemma? We must let God's Word renovate our thinking. Study the Bible's teachings on finances, and use a good concordance to help you. You might start by looking at what the book of Proverbs has to say about handling money and debt. Read what Jesus taught about giving and the priorities of money and possessions. God's Word is a unique and wonderful resource on handling finances responsibly!

The $64,000,000 (with inflation) Question

How can a supportive and loving wife help her husband cope with the financial pressures that are part of today's world? The best idea is to go to the book written by the divine financial planner. There is plenty of great economic advice in God's Word for all of us. A good place to start is Luke 12:13-31:

> Someone out of the crowd said, "Teacher, order my brother to give me a fair share of the family inheritance."
>
> He replied, "Mister, what makes you think it's any of my business to be a judge or mediator for you?"
>
> Speaking to the people, he went on, "Take care! Protect yourself against the least bit of greed. *Life is not defined by what you have, even when you have a lot.*" Then he told this story: "The farm of a certain rich man produced a terrific crop. He talked to himself: 'What can I do? My barn isn't big enough for this harvest.' Then he said, 'Here's what I'll do: I'll tear down my barns and build bigger ones. Then I'll gather in all my grain and goods, and I'll say to myself, Self, you've done well! You've got it made and can now retire. Take it easy and have the time of your life!'
>
> "Just then God showed up and said, 'Fool! Tonight you die. And your barnful of goods—who gets it?'
>
> "That's what happens when you fill your barn with Self and not with God" (MSG).

In reference to this passage, Dr. James Montgomery Boice wrote in his book *The Parables of Jesus,*

> There are not many places in the Bible where God calls people fools, so the fact that He singles out a preoccupation with things as folly is striking. In the Old Testament the man who says there is no God, that is, the atheist, is called a fool (Psalm 14:1; 53:1). So if that rich materialist is called a fool, it puts him right up there in the company of the God-deniers. In fact, there is an obvious

connection, for regardless of his intellectual opinions, the man who operates like the fool of Christ's parable is a practical atheist after all.[2]

Why does Dr. Boice refer to the rich fool as a "practical atheist"? He called him that terrible name because the man in the parable lived his life and conducted his business as though God did not exist. The foolish but wealthy farmer may have plowed the ground, sown the seed, tended the fields, and harvested the crops, yet without productive soil, water, and the sun all of his efforts would have been in vain. The farmer failed to rightfully give God the glory for his harvest.

As wise, faithful wives, we can heed the warning in this biblical picture and be quick to remember that God is the source of all we have. Even as we thank our husbands for all their hard work, we also need to glorify God for His provision:

> Beware that you do not forget the LORD your God.... Otherwise, when you have eaten and are satisfied, and have built good houses and lived in them, and when your herds and your flocks multiply, and your silver and gold multiply, and all that you have multiplies, then your heart will become proud and you will forget the LORD your God who brought you out from the land of Egypt, out of the house of slavery....Otherwise, you may say in your heart, "My power and the strength of my hand made me this wealth." But you shall remember the LORD your God, for it is He who is giving you power to make wealth....It shall come about if you ever forget the LORD your God...you will surely perish (Deuteronomy 8:11-14,17-19).

Everything we have ultimately comes from God's loving hand. He not only deserves our praise and thanks, He commands it! As we approach God in gratitude we can draw our husbands into the celebration of what God is providing.

When we realize that God is our ultimate provider, we can focus on what He wants for us. We can be content with all He's given us. And being content with what we have is essential if we are going to live happy, fulfilled lives. First Timothy 6:6-10,17 says it well:

> Godliness actually is a means of great gain when accompanied by contentment. For we have brought nothing into the world, so we cannot take anything out of it either. If we have food and covering, with these we shall be content. But those who want to get rich fall into temptation and a snare and many foolish and harmful desires which plunge men into ruin and destruction. For the love of money is a root of all sorts of evil, and some by longing for it have wandered away from the faith and pierced themselves with many griefs....Instruct those who are rich in this present world not to be conceited or to fix their hope on the uncertainty of riches, but on God, who richly supplies us with all things to enjoy.

The following is not only a lyrical commentary on one of the most foolish uses of money, but it well illustrates one of the many monetary snares our culture has set for the unwise ones who cry "Never enough!" or depend on chance or luck instead of God and His ways.

Play or Not
He's got bills coming due
And he sends the IRS his IOUs
He's got 21 years on a 10-year roof
But he gets in that line

He needs parts for his '68 Bel Air
Right now it's up on blocks, just sitting there
And there's holes in his daughter's shoes
She needs a pair
But it's his time
He's next in line

They'll put another Power Ticket
In the hands of the weak
And the ones who sell the dreams call it a game
But they won't tell him the truth
If he plays or if he don't
The chances he will win are still the same
Play or not, his chances are the same

He dreams of what will happen on that day
When the numbers drop, and they fall his way
But if he had every dollar he's already paid
He could buy those shoes
Pay some IOUs
He could bring that old Bel Air back from the dead
And the rain would be something not to dread
But the hunger for that game, it must be fed
It's what a fool would choose
You got to play to lose.[3]

Become a Funnel of God's Blessings

I have one more important suggestion about what you can do to help your husband find peace when it comes to the burdensome issues of money. This truth is summed up in Luke 6:38: "Give, and it will be given to you. They will pour into your lap a good measure—pressed down, shaken together, and running over. For by your standard of measure it will be measured to you in return."

Why is this passage so timely? In any culture where wealth is enjoyed there are two spiritual enemies that will fight for the hearts of its people. They are greed and discontent. The Luke passage is important because it offers one of the best weapons against this pair of foes that so many of us face. That weapon is *liberal giving*.

It's tough to be greedy when we make ourselves funnels for funds instead of fleshly piggy banks that get fat by feeding on the coins of discontent. Establishing a lifestyle of giving can empty our coffers before they become emotional and spiritual coffins.

Help your husband know financial peace by taking your monetary cares to the Prince of Peace and not being afraid to give liberally to God's work. And to further comfort your husband's heart, tell him something I heard a wise woman say: "God is a gentleman. If you give too much, He'll give it back!"

6

I Want My Husband to Know

I Will Show Love to His Family

NOT LONG AGO A FRIEND sent me an e-mail entitled "Men's Thesaurus." It contains some lighthearted illustrations of how men can say one thing and mean another. Some of my favorites are . . .

A man says, "May I help with dinner?" What he really means is: "Why isn't dinner already on the table?"

A man says, "Take a break, Honey, you are working too hard." What he really means is: "I can't hear the game over the vacuum cleaner."

A man says, "That's interesting, Dear." What he really means is: "Are you still talking?"

A man says, "Oh don't fuss, I just cut myself. It's no big deal." What he really means is: "I have actually severed a limb but will bleed to death before I admit that I'm hurt."

A man says, "I can't find it." What he really means is: "It didn't fall into my outstretched hands, so I'm completely clueless."

A man says, "What did I do this time?" What he really means is: "What did you catch me at?"

A man says, "It would take too long to explain." What he really means is: "I have no idea how it works."

A man says, "You know I could never love anyone else." What he really means is: "I am used to the way you yell at me, and I realize it could be worse."

A man says, "You look terrific." What he really means is: "Please don't try on one more outfit. I'm starving."

A man says, "I'm not lost. I know exactly where we are." What he really means is: "No one will ever see us alive again."

There was one more on the list that especially caught my attention:

A man says, "Guess what, Honey! My mom is coming to visit for a whole week!" What he really means is: "Please don't hurt me!"

Though it is true that when a young man and woman marry there are entire families being blended, it is amazing how little time the couple spends talking about this phenomena during their dating and engagement period. Among the many facets of an upcoming marriage that usually gets discussed are where the couple will live, how many kids they might want, their work, where to worship, and dealing with friends. Add to that list the endless number of details involved in planning the wedding day, and the in-law subject can be driven completely out of sight. But its importance is dangerously underestimated.

No matter how many times a couple is reminded that they are not marrying an individual, but they are actually uniting their lives with an entire family, it's still difficult for them to believe it. I confess that as far as I can remember, Steve and I never discussed the in-law issue. Maybe it was because we believed that both our families were wonderful and there was no cause for concern. Whatever the reason, we had no idea how much our union would be impacted by the influence of our immediate relatives.

Why is the issue of in-laws so difficult to deal with? It's because each individual family is jam-packed with unmovable traditions, unwavering opinions, and resolute ideas. Most families have strongly held convictions on everything ranging from how to fold towels to whether or not there is a doggie heaven. A friend of mine described the struggle she had in the beginning of her marriage when she tried to mesh with a family who had a different culture and a whole new set of rules:

> When I met my husband we were students in college. I was from New Jersey, and he was from Mississippi. I found his Southern manners and country drawl absolutely irresistible. He thought I was fascinating— different than any girl he'd ever met. I was more talkative and demonstrative than the other young ladies he had dated from back home. My take-charge attitude and bold ambition captured his heart. Everything was great until he took me home to meet his folks.

> From the beginning of our visit I was a little taken aback. I had not planned on a reenactment of the Civil War. Since I was from "up there," they immediately tagged me a "Yankee." My open, loud, opinionated ways were appalling to them.

> When I first met his mother, I did what I would have done if I were greeting my own mother. I wrapped my arms around her and gave her a big hug and kiss. Her nonresponse was surprising and rather hurtful. Hugging her was like embracing a dead fish. Now, 25 years later, my in-laws love me and think I'm incredible. And I'm happy to say the feeling is mutual. However, that transformation from leery to loving didn't happen overnight—nor did it happen by mistake. There was

some real effort put forth on both sides of the Mason–
Dixon Line to bring this Yankee and those Southerners
together. I am thrilled to say that my mother-in-law and
I are now best of friends. Who would have ever thought
it could be this way?[1]

The Greatest Joy, the Biggest Challenge

One of the greatest joys I have experienced in the last few years is
having our family multiply by more than half. Our daughter, Heidi,
met her husband, Emmitt, the first day of college. We immediately
knew that he was a young man of incredible character and integrity.
The same assurance filled our hearts when our son, Nathan, found
the love of his life in Stephanie. We couldn't have been more pleased
to welcome the two of them into our family.

Then in January of 2005 our family was once again expanded
with the arrival of our sweet little granddaughter, Lily Anne. Heidi
and Emmitt blessed us with the first of what we hope is many grand-
children. Of all the wonderful things Steve and I are blessed to do,
of all the wonderful people we have been privileged to meet, no
pleasure can compare to the joy we experience when we get together
with our children and, now, their children.

While making plans to be with family holds delightful anticipation for us, I realize the same is not the case for everyone. For
some, the outlook grates on their emotions like sandpaper. This is
especially true when there are unresolved conflicts. That tension is
poetically described in the second verse of a song Steve wrote about
a family gathering at the home place during the Christmas season.

> Some cross the street to get here
> Some come from distant shores
> Some arrive in their latest success
> And some arrive in rusty Fords
> One may come in anger
> One may choose to stay away

But if they do
I think I know
How they'll spend their holiday[2]

I've heard it said that every family is normal until you get to know them. That statement is never truer than when discussing the topic of in-laws. The subject of the in-law relationship and how it affects a marriage holds a lot of interest for me. So much so, I spent several years researching and writing the book *The Mother-in-Law Dance: Can Two Women Love the Same Man and Still Get Along?* I found it surprising that even though conflicts between in-laws pose such a potential threat to the marriage union there are few books written on the subject.

We often hear jokes about mothers-in-law and sons-in-law and how terribly they can treat one another, but rarely does anyone dare broach the topic of mothers-in-law and daughters-in-law. After looking into it quite extensively, I came to the conclusion that the subject is often avoided because it is such a fragile and potentially volatile relationship. To illustrate how difficult the in-law relationship can be, consider this woman's story. She knows too well how everyday life can be impacted when two women love the same man.

When my husband and I got married, in my ignorance I agreed to buy a house right next door to my mother-in-law. In all honesty, this was not fair to either of us. Since things had not changed that much, my mother-in-law saw no need to alter how she related to her son. To my disadvantage, she didn't make the connection between her son getting married and her responsibilities coming to an end. The only thing different in her thinking was now that he was married he simply lived next door and not in the next room. That was merely a small inconvenience.

From the beginning there were absolutely no boundaries between the two homes. At her will, she would enter without knocking. Anytime she had an opinion, she gave it a voice. She picked which church we attended. She was outspoken about how we spent our money, where we went on vacation, and how we raised our children.

If I had been a mean wife and hateful mother, perhaps I could have understood her stepping in to rescue her son and his children. But the truth is, I did a wonderful job with my family. I took great pride in serving them and creating a loving environment in our home. Her criticisms were totally unjustified. There was no reason for her to treat me so badly.

I tried everything to gain her approval and respect. I learned to cook her recipes (sometimes they tasted better than when she cooked them). I grew a large and fruitful garden and shared the vegetables with her.

Since she didn't drive a car, I would rearrange my day so I could take her to the doctor when she had an appointment or needed medical attention. Putting my own schedule aside, every week I would drive her to get her groceries. But all of my attempts to show her love were met, at best, with cold indifference and, at worst, open hostility. After so many years of trying, I finally realized that trying to gain her love and acceptance was nothing more than an exercise in futility. Withholding her praise and approval was just her way of controlling me.

Sadly enough, she never offered me her love and affection, not even when she was dying. Even though I've never felt such pain and rejection, I eventually came to realize that she was the one to be pitied. She voluntarily cut herself off from someone who truly cared about what happened to her.

There was a twist to the competitive nature of my relationship with my mother-in-law that I find baffling even to this day. There were times when I got the feeling she was jealous of any affection my husband gave to me. It was as though she was in a romantic rivalry with me. Living day in and day out with such a person, I've concluded that there's probably not a more unattractive relationship than a jealous mother-in-law and an insecure wife.

Being a Christian, I was able to fight through the hurt feelings in order to keep my eyes on the goal. I couldn't let how she behaved change who I wanted to be. My objective was to be able to live in such a way that I could look myself in the mirror and see the image of Christ being formed in me daily. I once read, "We are never more like God than when we are forgiving a wrong." Well, God must have really wanted me to be like Him. He gave me many opportunities to forgive on a regular basis.[3]

Learning from her sad story, we need to look at the in-law relationship and see what we can do to avoid such hurt feelings and broken-down boundaries. For a husband to enjoy a tranquil, happy life there has to be peace between his wife and his family of origin. What are some basic ways you can love your husband through his parents?

Everyone Wants to Be Acknowledged

The first place to start building a close relationship between you and your in-laws or to strengthen what you currently have is to praise the contributions they made to the life of your spouse. I know this sounds obvious, but sometimes we overlook the conspicuous. Even if you don't think your positive attitude will be returned, express your thanks to your in-laws. Tell them in person, make a phone call, write them a card. Let them know you appreciate their hard work, diligence, and love for your husband.

What kinds of things can you share with your husband's parents? In my case it's easy to identify some contributions Steve's parents made. For example, they have given valuable advice and affirming words that encouraged him in many ways. They have spent untold hours of prayer and fasting on his behalf. Steve's parents also invested in other types of resources that helped him. They made sure he got a good education. (And from our own childhoods and experiences, we know the enormous effort and the emotional toll it takes to get a child through school!) Assisting with homework and making Steve follow-through on his school obligations required a lot of attention too.

Steve's parents afforded him opportunities to go to interesting places and enjoy new experiences. They tended to his spiritual growth by making sure they took him to church and exposed him to godly people. The way Mrs. Chapman put it, "We drugged our kids…we drug them to church every time the doors were open!" Within their power, they saw to it that Steve knew God and was introduced to Jesus.

While they would quickly say that what they did for Steve, as well as his sister, Jeannie, was what any loving parent would do for their children, I know the sacrifices they made. They deserve my thanks and appreciation.

I can almost hear some of you saying, "Wake up and smell the coffee! Not every parent is the idealized version of Charles and Caroline Ingalls from the 1980s television show *Little House on the Prairie*." You might report, "My husband is who he is today in spite of his family. If left up to his parents, he would either be in prison or dead. He was mistreated, neglected, abused, and abandoned by the very people who were supposed to protect and care for him. I have nothing but disdain for those people. And now you're suggesting that I show love and respect to them? Yeah, right!"

There is no doubt about it, some parents were terrible. Everyone knows that there are mothers and fathers who think only of themselves and push their children aside. Or maybe they had their own problems that interfered with their parental abilities. In situations where parents were more of the problem than the solution, what can you do?

Wisdom that is especially helpful in how to get along with difficult in-laws is found in Romans 12:14-18,21:

Bless those who persecute you; bless and curse not.

Rejoice with those who rejoice, and weep with those who weep. Be of the same mind toward one another; do not be haughty in mind, but associate with the lowly. Do not be wise in your own estimation. Never pay back evil for evil to anyone. Respect what is right in the sight of all men. If possible, so far as it depends on you, be at peace with all men....Do not be overcome by evil, but overcome evil with good.

If your husband has a relationship with his parents, focus on what they did right. Did they love him, albeit imperfectly? Did they stay in his life? Did they strive to provide for him?

When you deal with difficult in-laws, discuss the situation with your husband. Together you can establish some boundaries that acknowledge the relationship but won't cause you undue stress. For instance, instead of spending all Christmas Day with your in-laws, let them know ahead of time that you'll only stay one or two hours.

Everyone Wants to Be Appreciated

Whether your husband's parents were fully supportive of him or not, if he has an ongoing relationship with them, so will you. As I said before, a great way to create a solid, loving relationship with your in-laws is to let them know—sincerely—that you appreciate what they've done right in the life of your spouse. Perhaps your acknowledgment can be expressed through kind words that are spoken or written in a letter or card. This communication doesn't have to be elaborate or complicated. Here's an idea to get you started:

Dear Mother-in-law,

Thank you for being such a wonderful mother to your son, my husband. Because of your hard work I am blessed to be married to a wonderful man. You share experiences with him as his mother that I can never fully comprehend.

You ran to his side and comforted him in the middle of the night when a bad dream interrupted his slumber.

Holding back your tears so he wouldn't see you cry, you're the one who drove him to the hospital when he fell off the bike and broke his arm.

At his bedside you knelt and prayed with him each night and shared God's Word with him each morning before he ran off to school.

You helped him with his science project, sewed his Pilgrim costume for the Thanksgiving Day pageant, and nursed him back to health when he had the measles.

For every act of kindness you did, for every character-building word you shared with him, I am indebted to you.

One of my favorite ideas of how to show appreciation came from a woman who said from the first days of her marriage to her husband, her mother-in-law had given her fits. The in-law would interfere by offering unsolicited advice, interrupting family time with uninvited visits and generally being a pain in the rumpus. The wife complained to her husband and asked him to run interference. She tried confronting, conniving, and caving in to her mother-in-law's manipulative ways. Nothing helped.

Then one day the daughter-in-law decided to take a different approach. She began to acknowledge the mother with honor and respect. On her husband's birthday she sent her mother-in-law a dozen red roses with a card expressing her appreciation for her hard work and faithful love toward her son. To the wife's amazement, the mother-in-law began to back off. She started to treat the daughter-in-law with respect. She immediately started honoring the boundaries of the different families and ceased much of the irritating behavior that had plagued the wife's life.

The wife commented, "I believe all she wanted was to be acknowledged. She wanted someone to say, 'You've done a good job.' When

I did that, she acknowledged my position as his wife. I wish I had done it a lot sooner than I did."

Everyone Wants to Be Loved

Whenever we openly acknowledge the efforts of others and take deliberate action to express our appreciation, the end result is giving them a sense of being loved and accepted for who they are. When we act in loving ways toward our husband's family, we actually are giving our spouse a wonderful gift.

One of the sweetest things Steve ever did for me was to love my mom and dad. My folks were decent, hard-working people. They owned and managed a dairy farm all their lives. Mom and Dad raised six children from the money they made through the business. Though the retirement my parents managed to save for their later years was adequate, it didn't allow for a lot of extras.

Much to my amazement, there were countless times when Steve, without my knowledge or prodding, would send them what he called "folding money." These gifts cushioned their budget and helped them not worry about unexpected expenses that would pop up from time to time. Whenever Steve sent them money, I felt loved. Steve's love and provision for my parents was another way he found to love me.

I was especially moved when I realized how much Steve cared about my father's well being after he was widowed. For two-and-one-half years my father lived all alone in a house that had once rung with the laughter and clamor of raising a large family. Steve wrote his feelings in the lyrics of the following song and, once again, I saw the depth of love he had for my parents.

Man in Aisle Number Two

Dear friend of mine, I write you this letter
How have you been since your mother passed away?
No one 'round here will ever forget her
But I need to tell you what I saw today.

I saw your dad at the grocery this morning.
He was wandering lost down aisle number two.
We spoke for a while, I said, "How've you been doing?"
He said he was fine, but in his arms he held the truth.

'Cause, he had one TV dinner and a box of saltines
One shiny red apple and a can of beans
One small jar of coffee, the kind you make with a spoon
Dear friend of mine, are you coming home soon?

How quick he said "Yes" when I invited him over.
And he smiled when I said, "Suppertime, we'll set a place for three."
As I was leaving, I looked over my shoulder.
And I thought of how you'd feel if you could see

That he had one TV dinner and a box of saltines
One shiny red apple and a can of beans
One small jar of coffee, the kind you make with a spoon
Dear friend of mine, are you coming home soon?[4]

As you can imagine, Steve's lyric served as a special motivation for me to go often to West Virginia from our home in Tennessee to see my dad. After my father passed away, I was extremely grateful that Steve had encouraged me to go for the visits. It was yet one more way I felt loved by my husband.

As wonderful as my experience has been in regard to my husband's love for my family, I am painfully aware that the opposite is sadly true for far too many couples. I counseled with a young wife who had been married a couple of years. From the time she and her husband began dating, she knew there was a potential problem. Even though she and her husband came from very different backgrounds (she was from a metropolitan city, and he was a country boy), she was not concerned with the two of them being able to mesh their lives together. However, she had a lot of doubts about whether she could adjust to her husband's family.

When she described the contrasting lifestyles of their two families, oddly enough she didn't even try to disguise her uppity attitude and her downright snobbery when it came to her in-laws. Being raised a country girl, I found her objections offensive. It was hard to figure out why she couldn't appreciate the differences in her family and his without judging one as right and one as wrong. Somehow she was unable, or perhaps unwilling, to accept their country ways. For instance, she found her mother-in-law's style of home-decorating intolerable. She openly rejected their simple lifestyle of fishing, hunting, and gardening.

Even though she could not find any common ground to build a mutually respectful relationship with her in-laws, she did realize that the problem was not their fault. It was her lack of tolerance and acceptance that kept her from appreciating the two different life-styles. She said, "I don't like this side of me, but all I know is when we go to visit his parents, I can't get out of there fast enough."

I wonder how her husband feels about the blatant disdain his wife has for his family. When a wife rejects those individuals who helped to shape and mold her husband's life, what she is really doing is casting shame on him. Like it or not, this young wife is telling her husband that there is something inherently wrong with him. There is no way her husband can totally divorce himself emotionally from his family of origin—nor should he be asked to. From everything this young wife told me, her husband's family sounded like great people. The best gift this young woman could give her husband is to find a way to learn to love and appreciate his family. When a spouse chooses to love and honor her in-laws, she is affirming her mate.

God can help us love our husbands enough to find ways to live at peace with our in-laws. We can find wonderful ways to show them we appreciate them and that we want to love them even as we love our own parents. Granted, some families are more difficult to love than others, but, nevertheless, if we want to love our spouses fully, then we will make the effort to love their families. (If you want more encouragement and more specific help on how to get along with your mother-in-law, check out my book *The Mother-in-Law Dance*.)

Helping Your Husband Cope

If your husband grew up in a dysfunctional family, and the wounds haven't healed and are affecting his life, reach out to him with support and love. Regardless of the lousy job a mother or father may have done as a parent, there is hope for the child. Psalm 27:10 gives assurance to the person who has suffered loss as a result of a poor or nonexistent parental relationship: "For my father and my mother have forsaken me, but the LORD will take me up." That verse is God's assurance that He will not let us permanently suffer harm because of the sin of another.

In addition, no matter what kind of harm that may have resulted from poor parenting, there is further encouragement in Ezekiel 18:1-4,19:

> Then the word of the LORD came to me, saying, "What do you mean by using this proverb concerning the land of Israel, saying, 'The fathers eat the sour grapes, but the children's teeth are set on edge'?
>
> "As I live," declares the Lord GOD, "you are surely not going to use this proverb in Israel anymore. Behold, all souls are Mine; the soul of the father as well as the soul of the son is Mine....Yet you say, 'Why should the son not bear the punishment for the father's iniquity?' When the son has practiced justice and righteousness and has observed all My statutes and done them, he shall surely live."

What can we do to help our husband deal with the deficit of living in a home where his parents did him harm and not good? We can encourage him to become the man of God he was intended to be. Just because your husband's daddy did wrong, doesn't mean your man will be a failure. Just because his mother was not who she was destined to be, her choices do not seal his fate. We live with our own individual responsibility toward God.

Instead of his flawed, earthly father being the image of what he thinks a man is supposed to be like, encourage your husband to look to Jesus and pattern his life after Him. What did Jesus do when He was mistreated and abused? He forgave. Hanging from the cross, He looked down at those who were killing Him and prayed, "Father, forgive them; for they do not know what they are doing" (Luke 23:34).

When we choose to show mercy to one who does not deserve it, then the windows of mercy are opened up to us (James 2:13). When it comes to being a parent, we all need mercy and not judgment. No matter how wonderful a parent we might want to be, none of us is going to do it right all the time. Our parents were not perfect, and we will not be perfect. And to the great surprise of our children, they won't parent perfectly either. There comes a time when, as adult children, we must look at what our parents gave us, call it sufficient, and let God make the difference.

7

I Want My Husband to Know

I Will Support and Embrace His Hobbies and Friends

IN THE CONTEXT OF MARRIAGE, the matters of hobbies and friends are areas where the husband and the wife must be willing to work together toward a 50/50 compromise. It is potential death to their friendship if either the husband or the wife perceives the solution to be only a win–lose scenario. In other words, if the wife feels that when her husband enjoys a hobby or his friends she is losing and he is winning, then they are on the road to trouble. And the opposite is just as true. Ultimately, a mutually satisfying arrangement is a prerequisite if the husband and wife are going to find resolution in these issues.

The answer to this complex situation is not found in the wife cowing and "giving in" if she feels that her husband has an obsessive, out-of-control approach to his hobby or his connection to his friends. Nor is the answer found in a wife forcefully wielding a self-imposed power, vetoing the likes and dislikes of her husband in an attempt to control his life. Instead, if they cooperate with one another in an understanding way, then they both win.

At the ripe young age of 46 Steve began to enjoy riding the metal pony more commonly known to those of us who prefer the stability of four wheels as motorcycles. I consider motorcycles dangerous toys. I have a tendency to agree with those who call the machines "donor bikes"—deadly accidents waiting to happen. Though I am not a fan of motorized bicycles, the middle ground for the two of us was reached when we both realized some things. I understood it is not my place to "parent" my husband and that my inherent fear, though justified, should not rob him of his interest. Steve came to understand my reservations and made some concessions that I greatly appreciate. To calm my fears he has agreed to not ride his bike on the Interstate, in the rain, or after dark unless absolutely necessary. These simple compromises might seem silly to some husbands, but to me they were monumental. And they are very good representations of Steve's and my 50/50 policy when it comes to hobbies.

Another serious interest Steve has that also has its inherent dangers is one that many other wives have to deal with. That hobby is hunting. While I didn't initiate his love of the great outdoors, I did unknowingly create an obsession. It happened many years ago.

When Steve and I got married we were singing with the contemporary Christian music group Dogwood. Since we traveled from city to city singing and worked in the studio recording music projects when we were home, we spent every day, all day, together. There was little time and even less money for anything other than work.

Our second wedding anniversary was approaching so I went out shopping for a gift for Steve. I stopped by a local antique store (actually back then they called them "junk stores"). I came across something I had never seen. It was a compound bow.

It was no secret that Steve loved hunting. In his early teen years he was introduced to the activity, and I wasn't a novice when it came to the "fair chase." The men in my family had always hunted. I had feasted on many a meal of squirrel, rabbit, venison, and even ground hog. So I understood the love some people cultivate for chasing critters in the outdoors. When I saw the reasonably priced hunting bow I was knowledgeable enough to know that it was probably a "toy" Steve might find interesting. I paid the cash and left the store with what I thought was an anniversary present. What I didn't realize was that I had actually purchased a lifelong passion for my husband.

There was no way that I could have fully known my gift would fuel a burning obsession that would afford Steve untold hours of pleasure. And little did I know that his love for hunting would ignite a whole new career opportunity for him. Three decades and nearly a dozen books later, Steve has managed to turn his love for God's great outdoors into a vital ministry of encouraging other men who share the love of hunting and all things related.

Men need diversions from work and, yes, even home. As important as both areas are to a man, he still needs activities that serve as stress relievers. Though this is an undeniable fact, the underlying reality is that those activities in which men engage affect their marriages.

Recently I conducted an informal survey of wives. I asked them this question, "How does your husband's chosen hobby and choice of friends impact your marriage?" Here are some representative responses. Can you relate?

- When we were first married I was really intimidated by my husband's love of golf. When he would go off with his friends, I felt unloved and abandoned. But after all these years of being married to him I've come to understand he's not trying to get away from me. He just loves to play golf. I've learned to fill the time when he's away with things I love to do.

- We don't have any conflicts over my husband's interests because we do everything together.

- My husband's hobby is hunting. When we were first married it caused some friction because I felt he loved hunting more than he loved me. But as I've matured in our relationship I realized how selfish I was. Now I send him off to the woods with a smile and a "have a great time." I wish it hadn't taken me so long to learn that encouraging him in something he loves to do is just another way I can love him.

- As our relationship has grown we find that we want to

do more things together. So I've learned to do something I never thought I would enjoy—riding on the motorcycle with him—and he's learned to do things he didn't think he could master—ballroom dancing.

- My husband having hobbies frees me to pursue interests on my own.

- Sometimes I feel like I am in competition with my husband's friends. It seems like he cares more about what his hunting buddies think of him than my opinion of him. I feel like he puts his hunting before me and the kids.

- With both of us working and trying to raise a family, we have very little time together as it is. His hobbies take time and money we don't have.

- I wish my husband had activities outside. What he does every free minute is watch TV. I would love to spend more time together, but I refuse to live my life in front of the "boob tube."

- I feel resentful that my husband "makes" the time for his hobbies when I don't have time to do anything for myself.

- I've come to the conclusion that men think differently than women. When my husband is out playing golf, hunting, or fishing, he takes a mental break from his other responsibilities. When I take a simple aerobic walk, just for my health sake, I walk as fast as I can. I'm not trying to get my heart rate up. I'm trying to get back to the house as quickly as I can so I can start dinner. Why can my husband enjoy his activities so casually while I am thinking about what I have to do when I get home? Is this a man/woman thing or is it just me?

- Anything my husband does, he always overdoes it. Whether it's a hobby or work, he goes way too far. I feel frustrated and alone most of the time.

- My husband spreads himself way too thin. He devotes lots of time to his hobbies and friends. He doesn't consult our plans before making plans with his friends. Yes, there is resentment on my part. I always get the leftovers.

- I would never ask my husband to choose between me and hunting because I have a pretty good idea that I would not like his choice.

- I feel good about my husband having activities and friendships that are special to him. He works all the time. I think he needs a diversion from his stress-filled, hectic life.

Wisdom for Wives

As you can tell by the comments the women made, some are more at peace with their husbands and their chosen activities than others. It only makes sense that some men do a better job balancing their marriage and their hobbies. If a wife hates what her husband loves to do, then he's not doing it right. Keep in mind, ladies, that men have specific needs when it comes to balancing family, work, and hobbies.

Men Need Solitude

Often the hobby a man chooses fills a specific need. Steve spends a lot of time in his work talking to people and hearing their stories and concerns. After a while his mind becomes flooded with too much noise and his spirit cluttered with pressing concerns and unceasing demands. The quiet and aloneness of the woods offer a cherished oasis that allows him a chance to sort out and file away many of the responsibilities he carries.

Jesus understood the value of a man getting alone and allowing the tranquility to feed his soul. A touching account of Jesus' need for solitude is found in the book of Matthew. In the opening verses of the fourteenth chapter Jesus learns that His cousin and fellow minister had been murdered by the evil Herod. The beheading of John the Baptist was a personal and tragic loss to Jesus. He had loved John, the son of his Aunt Elizabeth, since their childhood. Verse 13 says, "Now when Jesus heard about John, He withdrew from there in a boat to a secluded place by Himself; and when the people heard of this, they followed Him on foot from the cities."

All Jesus wanted was a chance to get alone with His Father and be comforted by the Holy Spirit. But the people wouldn't let Him out of their sight. The next verse says, "When He went ashore, He saw a large crowd, and felt compassion for them and healed their sick."

It wasn't until late in the evening, after Jesus had multiplied the fish and loaves and fed over 5,000 men—not to mention all the women and children—that He was finally able to steal away and be alone. And if the humanness of Jesus needed solitude, surely it stands to reason that other people need it as well.

Men Need Friends

Not only was man designed to need to get away by himself to commune with his heavenly Father, but he also was made to need the friendships of other men. In 2 Timothy 2:22 we are reminded of how important friends are to our pursuit of holiness. The apostle Paul was warning Timothy that he must respond to temptation by fleeing from youthful lusts. However, like Paul often did, he not only gave a stern warning against bad behavior, but he also gave an alternative response to those temptations. Paul said flee from evil, but he went on to say "pursue righteousness, faith, love and peace." The third part to this verse is often overlooked. Paul tells Timothy to engage this pursuit for holiness with "those who call on the Lord from a pure heart." The Living Bible puts it this way: "Enjoy the companionship of those who love the Lord and have pure hearts." In order for Timothy to consistently make the right choices when it came to dealing with victory over temptation, he needed to have the support of those who were like-minded. Paul knew his young protégé would need some social and spiritual reinforcements.

We need to encourage our husbands to develop and pursue friendships with godly men who love the Lord, who run from evil and actively seek to follow after righteousness. Our husbands need good men in their lives. If Jesus needed or enjoyed friendships, so do we! One of the first things Jesus did when He began His public ministry was to select 12 men to come alongside Him. God designed us to need one another. As wives we can meet some of the needs our husbands have, but we can't meet them all. God is able to meet our needs in supernatural ways, of course, but most often He sends friends and other loved ones to help us.

Men Need Support from Their Wives

A good rule of thumb is, as one wise gentleman suggested, "If you work together, you should cultivate separate interests. If you work apart, you should find an activity you both can enjoy doing." When Steve and I were first married, I thought because he loved the out of doors I should try and enjoy being in the woods with him. So one beautiful fall day I decided I would go squirrel hunting with him. There we were sitting among God's glorious wonders of gold, red, and orange leaves. As we sat under a mighty oak waiting for the appearance of a passing bushytail, I softly whispered, "Let's talk about the renovation we're planning in the basement."

Steve slowly looked over at me and didn't say a word. Then he looked into the trees. I continued, "I think we ought to start with replacing the garage door with French patio doors. What do you think?"

Without turning his head again in my direction, Steve whispered back, "If we're going to hunt, we can't be talking."

And talk we didn't…except for one quick response that I just couldn't hold in. I tried to keep it at a whisper but my vocal cords vacillated between a whisper and a low guttural growl. "I can be quiet at home. I came out here to spend some time with you, not just to harvest some tree rats!"

Needless to say, we took the advice that the wise man had offered, and since we worked together all the time, we thought it best to cultivate a few separate interests. It has worked well for us and helped us keep needed equilibrium.

Most men are going to have diversions. Whether it is hunting, fishing, motorcycling, golfing, fixing cars, collecting coins, or any other activity that might offer a respite from the everyday grind of work and the responsibility of home life, they will probably pursue an outside interest. And they want to do it guilt free. With that in mind, one more way a wife can show her love and support for her husband is to let him know that she wants him to enjoy his hobbies and "free" time.

Unfortunately we wives sometimes question the amount of time and money our husbands spend on their pursuits. How can we remain upbeat and positive about their other "loves"?

Steve and I have worked out some compromises that help us support each other's outside activities. Maybe they'll help you and your husband find a good balance between marriage, family, and hobby times.

Finding a Balance that Works for Both of You

To assist husbands, Steve wrote an entire book that gives men ideas of how to establish workable boundaries for hobbies. And because Steve and I are officially "one" I can borrow from his hard work and share some of his ideas from his *Good Husbands' Guide to Balancing Hobbies and Marriage*. Many of these suggestions come from the template of Steve's passion for hunting, but you'll find the suggestions applicable to most activities. (I suggest that a copy of Steve's book be obtained and presented to your husband for further discussion.)

Be Fair with Money

Use the "Price-Tag Doubling" method. Steve calls this method the "quick fix" and guarantees this will be one thing that will definitely help a wife not hate what a husband loves to do.

One of the recurring complaints wives have in regard to their marriages and their husbands' hobbies is that their men are much too willing to spend money on their own activities. For that reason Steve offers husbands a great solution to this problem. He calls it "price-tag doubling." Here's how it works.

Whenever Steve wants to dip into the family budget for something for his hobby, he calculates the cost of an item at twice the price. For instance, if he is going to buy another dozen arrows for his bow (priced around $75) then he knows he needs to budget $150 for the arrows. When he purchases the arrows, he gets the exact amount out of the bank in cash and gives it to me. If the budget can't stand that kind of hit, then the purchase is either delayed until it can be made or he works within budget and only buys a few arrows. When Steve factors me into the equation, it deflects any resentment I might feel. Showing equality with the family money is simply the fair thing to do. As Steve puts it, a fellow needs to "buck up and doe the right thing!"

Equal Time

In the same sense that money is limited, so is time. I don't mind Steve taking time for himself, but he's careful to not neglect those individuals in his life who depend on him and need his attention. This was especially true when our children were small. Steve would do something I appreciated very much. He "earned" his time in the woods by spending equal amounts of time with the kids. For instance, if he knew he was planning on spending three or four hours on the lake fishing, then he planned ahead and spent that same block of time with the children *before* he went fishing. This gave me a chance to get away and have some time to relax. I didn't resent his time away from us when he was careful to not be selfish or neglectful. We found that it was best when he gave the children their time up front. He knew very well that there's hardly anything quite so disappointing to a wife than making a promise to her and then not following through.

Don't Let Your Leisure Be Her Labor

When a husband's play becomes a wife's work there's trouble in the camp. For example, Steve was home alone for a couple of days and planned to get some things done around the house that I was hoping he would do. However, because I was out of town he felt free to add a quick early morning trip to the local fishing hole before he tackled the domestic chores. He managed to land a few finned species, and he cleaned them in our kitchen sink. The bad news is he got distracted during the day and the gutted, butchered fish marinated for hours in the kitchen. When he picked me up at the airport and took me home, we walked into our house and hit the putrid wall of foul fish gut odor. It took me hours of work using nearly every bottle of cleanser I could gather to overcome the incredibly disgusting smell. However, the odor-saturated wallpaper reminded us for days that Steve's leisure had become my labor. His apologies were accepted, and it hasn't happened again...thankfully.

Don't Let Your Fun Become Her Fear

I'll never forget the day I returned home after a morning of errands and discovered that Steve had fallen out of a treestand while deer hunting. The tips of his guitar-playing fingers were scraped up and the inner parts of his legs and arms were shredded as a result of the tree bark abrasions he collected as he attempted to break his fall. His fun fostered my fear. Since that potentially fatal disaster, he has been careful to carry a cell phone with him to the woods. Thankfully, Steve has done as much as possible to squelch my apprehensions regarding the dangers related to hunting by checking in often, letting me know where he is going to be, and working hard to keep his promises regarding the projected time that he'll return to the house. I appreciate him catering to my desire to know he is safe.

Don't Mess with Traditions

In his book Steve included a very candid admission regarding a critical mistake he almost made as a hunter. Our daughter and her soon-to-be-husband chose the weekend of the Thanksgiving holiday to marry. The problem with that date, at least for Steve, was that gun season for deer began on the Saturday of that weekend. In his attempt to salvage the opening day hunt, he suggested he would go hunting (and take the groom!) Saturday morning. He said, "I just know we can be out of the woods in time for the wedding."

My response? "If you go hunting that morning, you'll never be out of the woods."

That was when Steve realized family events such as weddings, birthdays, anniversaries, funerals, graduations, and other holiday traditions were to be given priority over his hobby.

Steve goes into more detail and offers four more surefire suggestions for helping husbands enjoy their hobbies free of guilt in his book *The Good Husband's Guide to Balancing Hobbies and Marriage.* It's a great, helpful book for men!

Steve wrote the following lyrics after talking to a fellow angler. He had called his buddy to see if he wanted to go fishing the next day. Although his friend was tempted by Steve's offer, he made the choice to spend some time with his sweetheart. After 40-plus years of marriage, Steve's friend Zane has come to realize that the fish will always be there, but time with his wife is something to treasure. Now that's a man who has learned to enjoy his passionate hobby *and* maintain a passionate love relationship with his wife.

Bother My Baby

Don't have to work tomorrow
I wonder what I'll do
Maybe I'll go fishin' with a friend or two
There's at least a thousand faces
And places I'd like to see
But the best idea I've ever had just occurred to me

I think I'll stay home and bother my baby
I think I'll stay home and get in her hair
I think I'll stay home and bother my baby
And maybe if I stay home I'll get somewhere

I'll follow her into the kitchen
Just to see her walk
I'll call her on the telephone
Just to hear her talk
I'll go outside and ring the doorbell
Just to hear her say, "Come on in."
I'll play a little hard to get
And hope she lets me win.

'Cause I'm going to stay home
And bother my baby...[1]

8

I Want My Husband to Know

I Am Honored to Be the Mother of His Children

BEING A MOTHER WAS NEVER high on my list of priorities when I was growing up. Spending time tending to little ankle-biters and corraling knee-high cookie-snatchers was not what I considered a fun time. Unlike many of my friends, I never babysat, taught Sunday school, or worked in a daycare facility. If small children were around, I usually went somewhere else. In college my roommate told me that she was planning on a family that included 12 children. I told her she could have my quota.

When Steve and I got married, I thought it was with the agreement that we would never have children. However, Steve demonstrated that love can be a little forgetful. Not long after we got married I reminded Steve of our agreement that we would be a childless couple. He claimed no recollection of that conversation. At the time I was a little miffed at his sudden and convenient case of amnesia. However, looking back, I am eternally grateful that God eventually blessed us with two wonderful children. Our son, Nathan, and our daughter, Heidi, have filled our lives with great joy and satisfaction. Now, with the addition of two in-laws and a granddaughter, our hearts are overflowing with blessings.

Artist or Craftsman?

Recently I spoke to a young mother of a small baby boy. She told me that she feared she would not be able to do the job of mothering correctly because she didn't possess what she considered a "natural mothering instinct." She told me how she had never really felt comfortable being around small children. Her conclusion was that perhaps she wasn't cut out to be a mother. By virtue of the contented sleeping baby she held in her arms, I assured her that she was indeed up to the job of mothering her precious little one. She was doing something right already. "Your challenge," I said, "is not to become a mother, you've already done that. And the things a mother does are something that can be learned."

As we talked about the uphill climb this young mom was facing, my mind went back to the time when I too felt ill-equipped to mother. The insecurities she expressed were like hearing echoes from my own heart. How well I understand that some women are born with a desire to mother, while others of us must work a bit harder to cultivate the skills to build these little temples where God desires to reside. Some parents are like natural-born artists who develop their craft while others are craftsmen who develop the art.

Steve enjoys painting landscapes on canvas. He's never been to art school or formally trained as a painter. He's simply been granted a God-given gift with the use of a brush. Our home is decorated with lovely pictures that are brought forth from an innate ability that seemed to preexist in him. You might say he started as an artist and got better at the craft.

While I possess none of the enviable natural skills for creating scenes on canvas that Steve enjoys, I did manage to learn how to paint a landscape. I didn't do it with a brush and oils but with a shovel and spade. In my backyard is a garden that graces our spring and summer months with a canvas of colorful flowers. But I didn't start with an innate gift for gardening.

My inspiration to tackle this unknown world of foliage and firth came from my mother, who loved cultivating flowers and all things lovely. Until my mom passed away, I never even planted a petunia.

Wanting to follow in her footsteps, I decided I would try my hand at growing flora, even though I feared I possessed a poisonous thumb rather than a green one. Knowing nothing about plants or how to take care of them, I set out to become a gardener. After reading and studying about the different plant life that could survive in our climate, I started working on a masterpiece that comes alive several months of each year. Where Steve flowed into an artistic skill that came natural, I struggled (with some satisfying success) to craft the art of gardening.

I believe the very same dynamic can apply to parenting. While some mothers and fathers seem to waltz right into the role of parenting with an instinctive understanding of what to do and all the warm and fuzzy feelings that accompany the arrival of a tiny baby, others have to deliberately learn how to relate and care for their children.

Keep in mind that neither of these parenting techniques, whether they came easily or were acquired through an act of the will, is superior to the other. Both accomplishes the same goal. So if you have the natural inclination of mothering or you need to acquire the skills, know that you can be a good…and even a superior…mother.

What a Privilege and Joy!

Not long after Steve and I were married, we received the sad news that Steve's grandfather had passed away. I had never had the privilege of meeting Steve's extended family, so going back for the funeral was my first trip to Chapmanville, West Virginia. Yes, you read it right. Steve comes from Chapmanville, and it is indeed filled with Chapmans.

The funeral for George Stonewall Chapman was well attended. While there was a host of friends and neighbors present at the service, the majority of folks in attendance was his grandfather's immediate family. He and his wife, Easter, had produced eight sons and three daughters, so with all of them in the pews, as well as their spouses, children, and the grandkids, the church was filled with Steve's kin.

As I quietly observed those around me, the thought came to me, *This man will never die. His seed will live on in all these people. He is a part of them, and they are a part of him.* The thought that followed was totally unexpected and, to say the least, it gripped my heart: *Steve is also an honorable man. Like his grandfather, and his dad as well, he deserves for his seed to live on.*

As a result of the softening of my heart that day regarding having offspring, a couple of years later Steve and I were blessed with the first of our two children. I may have entered into the parenting scene with a bit more apprehension and reservation than some, but without question, our children have proven to be the best expression of Steve's and my love for each other.

I want my husband to know that I am blessed beyond measure to have lent my womb for the purpose of bearing his children. Today, with the advantage of hindsight, I can see that while parenting was far more demanding of my time and energy than I expected, it was also far more rewarding than I ever dreamed. I truly am happy and blessed to have co-reared our children with my wonderful husband.

I hope you feel the same way about your husband. Make sure you let him know!

Yes, parenting by far is the most difficult work you and your husband will ever tackle. Both of you will need to roll up your parenting sleeves and work together. Let your husband know that whatever skills he can bring to the "changing table" will be cherished because you need his contribution. Make sure your husband knows how vital his participation in child-rearing is to your kids... and to you personally.

I asked some wives to share what their husbands do right when it comes to parenting. Here are some of their responses:

- He spends quality and quantity time with his children.

- He's involved in our children's activities—games, recitals, art projects.

- He's a good spiritual example to our children.

- He's a good, nonjudgmental listener.
- He provides well for our family.
- He helps the kids learn responsibility.
- He shows love to our children.
- He is very consistent with discipline.
- He loves our kids and would protect them with his life.
- He laughs and has fun with the kids.
- He's patient and very understanding.
- He puts the kids to bed every night.
- He wrestles and plays with the children.
- He takes our daughter on a date each week.
- He prays with our children every night.
- He is willing to enter in-depth conversations about God and what we believe. No question and no subject is off limits.
- He leads family devotions every night.
- He is careful to not criticize our kids.
- When our children are struggling or misbehaving, he tells wonderful stories using scripture in such a way that it is relevant to the kids.
- He verbally praises and affirms the children in public and private.

How can you support your husband in his role as father and encourage him as a dad? Applaud his efforts. Verbally let him know that he's doing a great job. Let him know what he's doing right. Use the previous list as ideas of what to praise your husband for.

You can also encourage him to branch out and find other ways to spend time with the kids and let them know he loves them. Here are seven areas that you can help your husband excel at. The impact each one can have on the lives of your children is amazing and very often immediate.

A Great Dad Makes His Kids Feel Safe

One of the favorite memories our children have concerns what happened during the hundreds of thousands of miles we've traveled together as a family. Oddly enough, it's something we did when we thought they were unaware. Whether we were arriving home after a 25-day trip to Texas or just arriving at Grandma's house after a quick 8-hour journey, the children loved it when their daddy would pick them up and carry them into the house. That feeling of being transported by their father gave them a sense of security that follows them to this day. Even though we thought they were asleep, they were subconsciously aware that they were securely wrapped in their father's strong arms.

Now our children are grown and they haven't been picked up and physically carried for quite a few years. However, they know that they are still carried by their father in another, more important way. Each week since they were born, Steve has diligently and consistently carried his children to the heavenly Father. What comfort and security this has been to Nathan and Heidi! Since our travels have always been mostly from Friday to Monday, Wednesday was part of our weekend. So Steve decided years ago to set aside that day, dedicating it to praying and fasting for our children…and now their spouses and our grandchild. I sincerely believe that the good health and well-being our family has known is a direct result of Steve's diligence in this area. The covering of prayer has likely done more than we can fathom to create a safe, loving environment for our family.

Encourage your husband to begin his own regimen of prayer for your family. I offer you this lyric that he, and you as well, can use to jumpstart this idea, but also as an ongoing model for your own prayer time. Steve wrote it on an early Wednesday morning while sitting in the quiet of his deerstand and praying for our children.

Wednesday's Prayer

Father God, to You I come in the name of Your Son
I bring my children to Your throne, Father, hear my cry

Above all else, Lord, save their souls
Draw them near You, keep them close
Be the shield against their foes
Make them Yours, not mine

Give them peace in Christ alone
And in their sorrow, be their song
No other joy will last as long
Father, calm their fears

Guide their feet, Lord, light their path
May their eyes on You be cast
Give their hands a kingdom task
A purpose for their years

And as my flesh cries out for bread
May I hunger, Lord, instead
That my children would be fed
On Your words of life[1]

A Great Dad Lets His Children Know They Are Loved

Mothers often have an easier time telling their children they love them than dads. But it's important that children hear the words from both parents. Show your husband by example and gently encourage him to tell your kids how much they are loved. I love you is a powerful, affirming statement.

Letting our children know they are loved seems like an easy thing. However, it is difficult to give something if it has only partially been experienced or never been received. Some fathers have a history that didn't include safety and security. Nor did some receive the loving and affirming words they desperately needed. For a dad like this, passing on the gifts of safety and affirmation to his own children is especially challenging.

My mind goes back to a conversation I had with a woman from Alabama. She told me about the traumatic scene when her husband was standing beside the bedside of his dying father. The feeble old man was in a lot of distress as she and her husband stood looking on. Suddenly the dying father sat up in bed, looked at the husband, and said, "What's happening to me, son? What's happening?"

Then the father lay back down. The woman said that her husband ran out of the room, crying uncontrollably. She joined him in the hallway to offer him consolation: "It must be awful, Honey, to see your dad dying this way." As he gained his composure he answered her. "I'm not crying because he's dying. I'm crying because that's the first time he's ever called me son."

Oh, what a sad story! What a tragedy—the wasted time, the unspoken words, the unexpressed love between a father and a son. If there is breath, there is time. All parents need to find a way to love their children and let them know it with the words they long to hear. It is important for the father to say those words, so help your husband if he lacks the skill.

I encourage you to not be afraid to gently remind him from time to time that your children hunger for him to make audible his love as well as his acceptance and affection for them. While you may hesitate to suggest to your reserved husband that he say his love out loud, try it. I am convinced you can do it with great results. I witnessed a mom doing this very thing while at a women's conference via a cell phone conversation with her husband.

As she and I sat together at lunch she relayed to me that her son was newly away from home as a college student and that while she was at the conference her husband had gone to the city where their son was to visit him. As we were talking, her cell phone rang and she said, "It's my husband. Excuse me, I must take this call."

I could tell from her words that her husband was with their son at that moment. With a very sweet voice that was nonaccusing and yet very confident, she told her husband, "Make sure you tell him you're proud of him. Say it three or four times, and say it in more ways than one!" Her husband must have thanked her for her gentle reminder because as she ended her phone conversation she smiled and said to him, "You're welcome, Sweetheart." All the dad needed was her tactful prodding and her timely reminder, and with it, so much good was accomplished.

If your tender urgings for your husband to offer his words of love don't work or work only on occasion, here's another suggestion. Instead of going to him, go to your kids and point out to them all the ways you can think of that their dad might say he loves them— only without words. After you reveal his love for them in this way, ask your children to thank him with their words or in a letter. I don't doubt that there's a whole host of grown children who probably wished a mother would have done this for them, and there's a good reason I suggest the idea.

My father's generation was not much on flowery, mushy words. Survival was the name of the game. The pervasive thought was if you have food and covering, what else do you need? Using my dad as a model, Steve wrote the following song to honor a father's words of love that are spoken clearly through works of love. May I suggest that if your children are old enough to understand these lyrics, for the sake of your struggling husband it would be appropriate to read this song to your children. Teach the kids through this poetry that there are more ways to listen than with the ears.

Love Was Spoken

Before the sun came up daddy rolled out of bed
He'd go to work and that's how love was said
He'd spend his money that he made all week
To feed a hungry family—that's how love would speak

Love was spoken, though daddy rarely used the words
Love was spoken in everything he did; love was all we heard

On Saturday morning when a man ought to rest
Dad would work on the house, and that's how love was said

When Sunday came we were off to the chapel
Love was spoken so pure and simple

Saying love did not come easy
But we did not criticize
But we could hear him say he loved us
When we'd listen with our eyes

Yes, love was spoken
Though daddy rarely used the words
Love was spoken
In everything he did
Love was all we heard.[2]

A Great Dad Has Fun with His Children

Most dads know that if they're going to have children, they need to work and provide for their many needs. If you were raised in a home where your father failed to provide financially for the family, then you know what a hardship a nonindustrious dad can put on the children.

But a busy dad can sometimes be unaware that working to provide for his family is not the end of his responsibilities. A father needs to realize that his vocation is only one of the many components of being a great dad. Having fun with his children is on that list too. For some fathers, the best news they could ever hear is when his wife says, "Sweetheart, I want you to feel free to have fun with the kids. Be adventurous with them, make some memories…have at it with the fun stuff!" Why is this often the case? Because most men *want* to have fun with their kids—at least it was true for Steve and our children.

As an avid outdoorsman, Steve longed to take our kids on adventures in the wild. He couldn't wait until they were old enough to take along. Their adventures became some of the best memories they share together. Long hikes on the Appalachian Trail, fishing overnight way out in the remotes of the Gulf of Mexico, canoeing, kayaking, camping, and bicycling across country are just a few of the many things Steve did with Nathan and Heidi.

It might not be easy for you to let go of the kids to be with their dad in mountains where there are bears, seas where there are sharks, highways where there are cars whizzing by flimsy bicycles, and so on. A mother who encourages her husband to engage in the frivolity must face the fear that can go with it. But the outcome is twofold in benefits. Not only will the kids cherish the memories they make with their dad, the break for a busy mom that comes because the kids are away with Dad can be life-changing. As Steve says, "Annie always looked so refreshed when the kids and I would come home after being gone...for a year!" Seriously, a single day break worked wonders for me.

A Great Dad Is a Good Example for His Children

Finding positive examples for our children to follow is not that easy. But no one will influence our children more than us. Children tolerate a lot from their parents. They will accept their parents being:

- old-fashioned
- too strict
- totally wrong

But the one thing that fosters rebellion quicker than anything else in our children is when they detect hypocrisy. Our children long for us to be consistent and to walk what we talk. They need for us to live authentic, honest lives that they can copy. Steve wrote a song about his father and the wonderful example he was to him.

Daddy's Shoes

Daddy's shoes made a deep impression
In that West Virginia snow
I put my feet where he was steppin'
He made a real good trail to follow
And he led me home that winter day

Back in 1955
That was years ago
But I can say
That in this heart of mine

I'm still steppin' in the tracks
Of my daddy's shoes
It's a trail I love to follow
And it'll lead me through
When life turns cold and bitter
I just do what I saw him do
It'll lead me safely home someday
Steppin' in the tracks of my daddy's shoes[3]

Steve further commented that one of the most meaningful traits that his father had was that "what he was at home, he was at church, and what he was at church, Dad was at home." What an incredible testimony to the presence of integrity in a dad.

We want our husbands to know that if they didn't have a positive example to follow in their fathers, it is by no means too late to become to our kids what they never had growing up. Just as it is true that a farmer can sow certain crops in the autumn of the year (winter wheat, for example) and get a yield, our spouses can be encouraged that it is never too late to sow the seed of a good example in our children.

Let your man know you will support him as he sows those seeds. Remember, "we can't do anything about our ancestors, but we can certainly do something about our descendants!"

A Great Dad Shows His Children Courage

Not only does a dad make his kids feel safe, loved, and provide a good example, a great dad also demonstrates courage in the face of adversity. I watched as my father faced challenges on the dairy farm that would have killed some men. From the enormous financial burdens to the simple frustration of little annoying wintertime ice balls on the tip of a cow's switching tail, my dad braved the full range of difficulties that can weary a farmer.

Though the farm was always an uphill climb for my dad, perhaps the highest of mountains he had to climb was watching my mother courageously battle cancer for ten years before her passing. Amazingly, my dad endured all these physical and emotional obstacles with only 20 percent use of his heart for the last 28 years of his life. Watching him stand up in the face of the fierce weather that life's mountains generated has inspired me to be a more courageous person.

Steve observed courage and strength in his dad as well, but in a different way. Steve was raised in a pastor's home, and he was privileged to see a brand of bravery that required not only emotional control but the necessary fortitude to restrain the tongue in those trying times. Those "opportunities" came when his dad (and mother, too) were unjustly treated by those who were enemies of their ministry. His folks responded to adversity with great love and the strength of dignity.

One of the fiercest battles Mr. and Mrs. Chapman faced is described in the following story.

Don't Unpack Your Bags
The new preacher walked upon the porch
Knocked on that old screen door
Waited until the light came on
Said, "Good evening, ma'am, I'm Pastor John
I just stopped by to say Hello
Take a minute and let you know
I just came here to your fine town
And I start next Sunday morning"

She stepped out in the evening air
Sat down in an old oak chair
Said, "Young man you seem so nice,
But could I give you my advice?
Preachers have come to that church for years
They've come with smiles, but they leave with tears

One by one, like a sad parade
And I offer you this warning.

"Touch a feather to their ear
Tell them what they want to hear
Give them milk, don't give them meat
Make it short and make it sweet
If you want to stay around
That's what you'll have to do
But don't unpack your bags, young man,
If you plan to preach the truth!"

She said, "I don't go to that church no more
There's dark behind those doors
First time they rang that steeple bell
They must have heard it down in hell

"'Cause they sent their minions to that place
And they hide behind the human faces
Of those who would trade your soul and mine
For just a taste of power."

She said, "Now you may wonder how I know
It's 'cause a preacher came here years ago
I loved the way he shined the light
On what was wrong and what was right
We fell in love and we planned to walk that aisle
But they tore him down and stole his smile
He carried that pain to an early grave
It's been hard to be forgiving

"So you better…touch a feather to their ear
Tell them what they want to hear
Give them milk, don't give them meat
Make it short and make it sweet
If you like this little town, that's what you'll have to do
But don't unpack your bags, young man,
If you plan to preach the truth"[4]

The courage Steve's dad showed his son as he refused to let someone else's bad behavior change him modeled a fearless pursuit of integrity that impacted the lives of both his children. Let your husband know that the same can be true for him and your children as well.

A Great Dad Is First a Great Husband

Perhaps one of the greatest temptations for parents is to forget that their first priority is their roles as husband and wife. This oversight is easily made in the face of a mountain of diapers, a warehouse full of baby food jars, rooms that look like an explosion of toys took place, and a backseat of a car that has no room for adult passengers because of the car seats. As time progresses, it's tough for dads and moms to find time for romance while running by each other through the kitchen, hurrying to jobs, school, dentist and doctors' offices, ball fields, and on and on. In the business of parenting, it's especially important for husbands and wives to remember: "We're not just mom and dad, we're lovers too!"

Let your husband know that anytime he wants to disappear for an hour or a day, you'll do all you can to "run away" with him. Let him be aware that even when the kids resist your occasional absences, you'll go anyway and harmonize as he sings the following anthem of determination:

Before There Was You

Children, please give me your kind attention
I've something to say; here's my intention.
I'm gonna go out with your mother tonight
No, you can't come,
It won't help if you cry.

Oh, you may wonder
How I could be
So heartless to want
Just your mother and me

She's your dear mother,
I know that it's true
But she was my sweetheart
Before there was you

First we'll walk by the ocean
And we're gonna hold hands
We'll write our names
In the wet sand
We'll write, "I love yous"
Send them off in a bottle
Then in memory of you
We're gonna eat at McDonalds![5]

A Great Dad Knows the Heavenly Father

Finally, there's no way to measure the depth of impact that a father can have on children's hearts when he leads them spiritually into a relationship with Christ. It is my prayer for my husband that when his name is formed on our children's tongues that a certain sweetness accompanies it. It was that kind of fondness for his grandfather that inspired Steve to write the following song. May the spirit of this lyric be present in the hearts of your children whenever they mention their father's name.

One Man Prayed

Back behind me on the trail of time
There's a place that is sacred to me
Sometimes I go there in my mind
And I look upon it thankfully

'Cause it was there, long before my years
That a man whose blood runs through my veins
Fell on his knees and he said with tears
"God save my soul in Jesus' name."

That was the place
That was the time

When amazing grace
Came into my bloodline
And my soul was forever changed
'Cause one man prayed
In Jesus' name.

If time goes on further down the trail
Others will be born, then born again
And if I'm around I'll be sure to tell
How it came to pass that grace came in.[6]

9

I Want My Husband to Know

I Respect Him

IT IS HARD TO DESCRIBE how awkward it feels to be in a social setting with a couple who are at odds with one another and who do nothing to conceal it. I'll never forget the uncomfortable situation Steve and I experienced when some friends of ours began to exchange barbs and jabs across the dinner table from us at a crowded restaurant.

Every couple has moments when the effects of fatigue, frustration, hormones, or even a general state of irritability result in an occasional isolated conflict. And, granted, it can sometimes be very difficult in those moments to rein in the tongue and keep sharp words from becoming lethal weapons. But the drawn-out dinnertime drama that our good friends were providing for all in earshot suggested there was something deeper at work than just being momentarily edgy with one another. They went from a flash of hot temper to a forest fire of rage.

The bitterness between the couple became far too obvious to overlook when the tone of their conversation turned painfully personal. As if she knew exactly what target to hit in order to do the most damage, the wife began to give cutting, unsolicited commentary on her husband's passion for competing in marathons.

Through long hours of training and unabated determination, he had become a runner extraordinaire. However, his wife expressed anything but admiration as she continued to lob stinging salvos across the table. The tablecloth was spattered with emotional blood that ran from the wounds in his ego. Sadly, they were deep gashes that she was deliberately inflicting in him.

Steve and I wanted to crawl under the table when she began to loudly taunt him. She called him, of all things, a "skinny running stick." The look on his face was at first pitiful as she laughed and poked fun at something he obviously took great pride in doing. However, his expression eventually changed to a mixture of anger, embarrassment, and utter disgust. As quickly as we possibly could, we changed the subject and managed to make it through the evening, even as the sourness between them became increasingly bitter.

We were horribly saddened about the incident, and it didn't surprise us when we heard later on that the husband had left his wife. Nor did it surprise us that he left her for a woman he met at the running track where he regularly trained. Eventually we learned that the woman for whom he gave up his long marriage, as well as a very impressive job, didn't withhold her admiration for his dedication to fitness and his love for "the long race." He not only sacrificed an enviable position of authority at his work in order to move to another city with the other woman, he willingly abandoned his relationships with his children for the sake of the attention his "new interest" was ready to give him.

While the full blame for their break-up might not rest totally on the shoulders of the abandoned wife, we were convinced that one of the major contributors to the husband's behavior was his wife's unwillingness to offer her husband the respect he hungered for. Had she fed that need in his soul, they might still be together today.

The need for a man to be treated respectfully is brilliantly explained in the insightful book, *Love and Respect.* The author, Dr. Emerson Eggerichs, said:

> In one national study, four hundred men were given a choice between going through two different negative

experiences. If they were forced to choose one of the following, which would they prefer to endure?

- to be left alone and unloved in the world
- to feel inadequate and disrespected by everyone

Seventy-four percent of these men said that if they were forced to choose, they would prefer being alone and unloved in the world....

For these men, the greater negative experience for their souls to endure would be to feel inadequate and disrespected by everyone. I have had numerous men confirm this research by telling me, "I would rather live with a wife who respected me but did not love me than live with a wife who loved me but did not respect me."

While my heart ached for our friends, and particularly for the wife who was left alone, I saw her dilemma as my cue to examine my own heart as a wife. I honestly asked myself, "Am I showing sufficient respect to my husband? The kind that will feed the hunger in his soul and ward off any disappointment he faces or, worse, any thoughts of leaving?"

I knew that to find the true answer I had to be willing to ask the one who could best provide it. I had to ask Steve. I also knew very well that if I thought about it too long I might let the inherent risk of asking such a question cause me to remain silent. So I went straightway and said to my guy, "Do you feel respected as my husband?"

I was both amazed and relieved that he answered with hardly a hesitation. "Yes, thankfully I do." I can't tell you how grateful I felt to hear his affirming answer. I didn't doubt my respect for him; it was simply a joy to know that he recognized it. Then curiosity urged me to probe a little deeper.

Feeling a little more confident I further inquired, "How do I show you respect?" His response was not as quick as before, and I got a bit worried. However, after about 15 seconds of total silence, he said, "Let me think about it, and I'll write it down for you."

I happily said, "That's fine—and take your time." I wanted to hear all he would offer. Little did I know what encouraging words would pour out of his pen. About 45 minutes later I got the following hand-written response.

> Dear Annie,
>
> Let me say first that I live with a quiet dread that I would somehow lose your respect or admiration. I would honestly feel devastated, worthless, and unaccomplished if I sensed that you had no respect for me. To not have it would be a sure sign that I have done or am doing something terribly wrong. If you haven't noticed, I long deeply for your respect. And, thankfully, I do feel like I am blessed to have it. I am profoundly grateful.
>
> As for the things you do and say that are signs of your respect for me, the list is long so I'll mention only a few. I suppose you'd like to know their order of importance, but to be honest, each of them belongs on the first line. I'll simply list them as I think of them. So here goes…
>
> The way you have accepted and loved my family and my heritage, the unwavering devotion you have shown to caring for our two children (and now their mates and kids), how you tend to our home and house, and the sweat you have invested in caring for the material things we steward, are signs of your respect for me. Your encouraging comments about the work I do and how you faithfully stand beside me as a co-laborer, your acceptance of the play I enjoy, your carefulness with money and the way you share my disdain for debt—these things tell me you respect me.
>
> When you don't laugh at my fears (like flying), the fact that you don't, nor have you ever, laughed at my physical imperfections, and how you challenge me to a higher moral standard by wisely (yet tactfully) refusing to laugh at some of the things I find humorous. These things tell me you respect me.

Seeing how you choose friends who enhance your character and not tear it down tells me you care about your own character. I see that as respect to both me and to "us." And I feel admired when you are brave enough to tell me (and you always do it with godly diplomacy) that you discern something questionable in a person I might see as a potential friend. That kind of challenge is a sure sign that you care deeply for me, and I interpret it as an abiding respect.

I probably don't show it, or if I do I don't do it well, but I burst with pride when I hear you say to others in public that you are proud of me or that I have done or said something that you find amazing. To be honest, this one might be one of the top signs that I have gained your respect. And let me say, I think I know you well enough to believe that when you verbalize such nice things in the presence of others, you are not patronizing me. Thankfully, you're not that way. I wouldn't want you to be that way. But because I am convinced that you say those things only because you mean them, it makes it doubly delicious to my soul.

And there are little things that amount to big respect, such as when I go to my chest of drawers and there are clean skivvies, socks, and T-shirts that I know didn't get there on their own. When you let the car engine warm up (at my request) on a bitter cold winter day. And on the subject of food, when I smell the "healthy cookies" (with oatmeal, nuts, and raisins) baking in the oven, the pot of Santa Fe soup on the stove, the meat on the grill, or when you smile and break out the bag of home-prepared food while we're riding on yet another airplane, I feel respected (and really happy!).

There are incredibly important things you do that I see as respect, like your faithful devotion to God's written Word. And I am honored by your readiness to share your knowledge of the Scriptures with me. It inspires me spiritually, and I see it as a true and blessed sign of your respect for me.

I also know that you talk to Him about me in prayer. It's a mystery too hard to explain, but I can honestly sense the effects of your petitions to Him on my behalf. And I know that there are even those times when you ask Him to change my mind about something instead of trying to do it on your own. I really appreciate it that you care so much about my spiritual condition that you would quietly include me in your conversations with God and trust Him with the outcome.

And I would be sadly remiss if I didn't add one more thing. Your own spiritual journey that led you through the sorrows of your younger years to the wholeness that God alone has given you to display today, and the fact that you still let Him help you maintain that strength and integrity, is the ultimate sign of your respect for me. Why? Because I know, without a doubt, that your intense gratitude for the Savior's grace that was shown to you is the one thing that motivates you most to help me know Him better each day.

The way you cherish your relationship with the Lord tells me that your greatest hope for me goes far beyond the temporal and reaches forward to the eternal. It says to me that you love and respect me enough that you want to do all you can as a wife to create and keep an environment in our home where God is welcome to help me grow in His grace. I don't doubt for a moment that the reason you want me to know Him well is so that on that coming day when we all stand to be judged in His holy presence, I can do so with confidence in His righteousness alone that redeems me.

Finally (for now), your desire that I be with you in heaven as forever friends to celebrate the One who made us one here for a time is, my dear Annie, the sweetest sign of your respect for me...and I humbly thank you for it. Steve

When I finished reading Steve's response, needless to say, I was overwhelmed. And as I sat with him, as most wives might do, I alluded to the possibility that he might have overstated things a bit. He looked at me with that "it's a compliment, take it and enjoy it" expression. He assured me that he meant every word on the paper. I was humbled by the fact that in the everydayness of life, in the midst of simply trying to be a good wife to him, I never dreamed I was doing all that he had listed. I fear that if I tried to consciously do those things he mentioned I would fall horribly short. Yet to deliberately express my respect to him is precisely what Ephesians 5:33 is admonishing wives to do. The passage says to women, "and the wife must see to it that she respect her husband." The instruction to *"see to it"* is not something that happens accidentally. It requires an "eyes wide open" approach to showing respect. To close my eyes to my husband's need for respect can result in actions and words that may make him feel rejected.

As you think about the ways you respect your husband, bear in mind that it's often the "little" acts that happen daily that assure your man that you truly honor him.

Very often when a man feels rejected instead of respected, his emotional response is anger. For that reason I asked several hundred women this question: "What is one thing you do that makes your husband angry?" What I ultimately wanted to know was, "In what ways do you show disrespect to your husband?" I had a feeling that if I asked wives such a straightforward question, they might not recognize the actions that can indicate disrespect. No woman who truly cares about her husband would deliberately do anything to make him feel unloved and disrespected. Yet, as you will see from the responses offered, that is exactly what many of us do—whether we realize it or not.

- I don't follow his advice or instructions.
- He gets upset when I make him account for money he spends.
- He hates it when I comment and give an opinion before I know all the facts.

- He gets angry when I complain about his work. He feels pressure from me to be home even when his workload demands he work longer hours.

- When I confront him with issues he doesn't want to talk about he gets irritated with me.

- He hates it when I interrupt him during a conversation because I think I know what he is talking about and I have my answer ready.

- He hates it when I give all my effort at work and then neglect the house and bills. He feels like I care more about everyone else than I care about him.

- He gets angry when I tell him he's wrong and I'm right.

- He hates it when I keep repeating what is bothering me, even after he thinks the conversation is over.

- He gets very angry when he feels like I'm not listening to him.

- He gets really angry when I try to control everything, even down to the smallest detail.

- He gets angry when he thinks I am lying to him.

- He gets very upset when I accuse him of being unfaithful, even when he's not.

- My husband gets angry when I criticize and put myself down.

- The thing that makes my husband the most angry is when I act like I don't care about him.

- My husband yells, but I give him the silent treatment. This makes him really mad.

- When I hound him for more information he gets upset with me.

- My husband gets angry when I volunteer too much and

don't leave enough time for us. I think he feels unimportant.

- My husband gets angry when I argue with him.

- He gets angry when I overrule him when he's trying to discipline the children. To disagree with him in front of the children really makes him mad.

- He gets upset when I withhold words of affirmation.

- My husband gets angry when I tell him he reminds me of his father. His father is an abusive man.

- He gets angry when I say "We shouldn't have gotten married." I think it hurts his feelings, but he reacts with anger.

- My husband hates being nagged when he's driving. He has no sense of direction, and I feel like I have to tell him every turn to make.

- He gets upset when I try to keep him on schedule. He tells me I'm his wife, not his secretary.

- My husband gets angry when I tell him he doesn't do enough for our family.

- My husband gets very angry when I call my mom and tell her about our problems.

- He gets angry when I withhold sex.

- The littlest things can set my husband off. He gets really angry when I leave doors and drawers open and lights on in the house.

- My husband hates to go to bed alone. I like to stay up late. This is a source of conflict between us.

Do any of the women's admissions sound familiar to you? Are you guilty of being disrespectful to your husband in ways you define as "making him angry"? If you have indeed said or done things that have fostered or are currently generating your husband's anger, please don't lose heart. There is good news! You can begin today to change the landscape of your marriage by feeding your husband's hunger for respect. And there's even better news. There is a very convenient place for you to start. It's called home:

> Home is the most important place for a man to be affirmed. If a man knows that his wife believes in him, he is empowered to do better in every area of his life. A man tends to think of life as a competition and a battle, and he can energetically go duke it out if he can come home to someone who supports him unconditionally, who will wipe his brow and tell him he can do it. As one of our close friends told me, "It's all about whether my wife thinks I can do it. A husband can slay dragons, climb mountains, and win great victories if he believes his wife believes that he can."[1]

Without question, a wife should consciously strive to find ways to show respect and admiration to her husband. The specific instruction that God gives to women to "see to it that she respect her husband" is as much an unconditional decree as the command God gives to husbands to "love your wives, just as Christ also loved the church and gave Himself up for her." These demands to love and respect are not optional nor seasonal.

For those wives whose challenge to demonstrate respect for her mate is made extra hard by the conduct of their husbands, know that you are not alone. I asked women, "What can your husband do to help earn your respect for him?"

- If he were more kind and patient with others then I would respect him more. It's hard to respect someone when you see he shows no respect to others.

- I would respect my husband if he were more open to new ideas. A closed mind is very unattractive.

- If he would listen to me and understand my concerns then I would be more willing to listen to him. His lack of respect for me causes me to pull back from him emotionally and in every way.

- My husband needs to validate my feelings. My heart would be more willing to consider his needs and wants if I thought he cared about me.

- I find it hard to respect my husband because he has no relationship with God.

- I would respect my husband more if he would learn to handle tense situations with kindness and diplomacy.

- I would respect my husband more if he cared about me and was willing to consider what I want to do once in a while.

- I would respect my husband more if he would help me around the house. My home is important to me, but he doesn't seem to care if things are nice or not.

- I would show my husband respect, if he would show love for me.

- If my husband were a spiritual leader in our home then I would be more willing to listen to him and show him respect. [This was the most common response from the women. Many of them lacked respect for their husbands because their husbands failed to show spiritual leadership in the family. I don't think men really understand just how important being a spiritual leader is to the women.]

- I would respect my husband if he would make the effort to put his family first once in a while. It seems like he never spends time with the family. I think his priorities are all messed up.

- I would respect my husband if he would control his tongue and not use words to cut me down.

- My husband is emotionally abusive to our children. Until he changes his behavior toward them, I can never respect him.

- I would respect my husband if he would do a better job at his work. I think he's lazy and doesn't work as hard as he should.

- Basically my husband just needs to grow up and be a man.

- I would respect my husband if he would be more sensitive and be more gentle with me. I really need him to listen to me.

- I would respect my husband if he would stop his childish tantrums. He needs to control his hot temper.

- It would be a lot easier to respect my husband if he would be willing to apologize when he's wrong.

Where do you go for help when you aren't showing respect for your husband and the Bible says you should? Whether the challenge is made more difficult because of your pride or the bad behavior of your spouse, the source of strength to do the right thing is found in God's Word. And there's a very good reason why the Scriptures offer such hope.

Hebrews 4:12-13 reminds us that "the word of God is living and active and sharper than any two-edged sword, and piercing as far as the division of soul and spirit, of both joints and marrow, and able to judge the thoughts and intentions of the heart. And there is no creature hidden from His sight, but all things are open and laid bare to the eyes of Him with whom we have to do." It is God's Word working in and through us that gives us the power to change. For a more fulfilling and happier marriage, your husband needs to know that he's important to you and you respect him. This doesn't mean you expect him to be perfect in all areas. Focus on what your spouse does right or well.

With the changing power of God's Word as our hope, consider the joy that a couple can experience if they adhere to the instruction given in Colossians 3:12-15. Though this admonition is given to the church, it is wisdom that can apply to the simplest expression of the church—the husband and wife union:

> Put on a heart of compassion, kindness, humility, gentleness and patience; bearing with one another, and forgiving each other, whoever has a complaint against anyone; just as the Lord forgave you, so also should you. Beyond all these things put on love, which is the perfect bond of unity.

Notice that the passage says "put on" those things that can literally change the tone of relationships. That phrase *"put on"* sounds very similar to "see to it." Once again we are asked to deliberately act in ways that will bring peace into our relationships. There will be times when it takes intentional action, specific mental effort to avoid acting or reacting in ways that can make a husband feel disrespected. Even if the effort to follow this Colossians wisdom is one-sided on your part, you will reap benefits for following God's admonition. I know it won't always be easy. I'm reminded of the time I realized my tendency to blame Steve...

> When we left our hotel in Fargo, North Dakota, we had plenty of time to make our flight to our home in Nashville through Minneapolis, Minnesota. Facing a long, boring travel day that included an unwelcome three-hour layover, we were taking our time checking in with the ticket agent at the Northwest counter in Fargo. The agent looked at our ticket then taking a closer look at her computer screen, she said, "Did you know that there is an earlier flight that would get you to Minneapolis just in time to connect to an earlier flight to Nashville?"
>
> Nothing could have perked us up more than hearing we could

avoid another laborious delay. "Really?" we eagerly replied. "How much sooner could we get to Nashville?" Her response sent us into a whirlwind of activity. Our ultra-conservative time allowance had given us just the open window we needed to catch the earlier flight if we hurried. With the steely nerves of seasoned travelers we began the mad rush to the gate to make the earlier flight.

We would have been fine going through the security check if we had been just a minute earlier. For some reason the family in front of us triggered the security bells and whistles. Each member of the family had to be searched. Each carry-on bag had to be emptied and thoroughly gone through. The family didn't look dangerous to me, but there must have been something about their tickets that set off the TSA agent.

What would have been no problem with our original schedule now became a heart-thumping, head-throbbing, nail-biting situation. Our window of opportunity to catch the earlier flight was quickly closing.

Finally we were allowed through the metal detector and smoothly passed the scrutiny of the attentive guards. Steve was still trying to get his shoes and jacket on when I took off in a mad run. I reached the departure gate just as the agent was ready to close the door to the Jetway. As I was pleading for mercy, Steve finally appeared at the top of the escalator.

The gate attendant took our boarding passes, and before long we were safely on board our flight. Even though sweat was dripping off our foreheads, and we were disheveled and distracted, we gratefully sat down in our seats.

Nearing the end of our flight I began to collect my belongings. For some reason I opened up the little pouch in front of me to take a look at the complimentary magazine offered by the airline. When I glanced at the periodical something familiar caught my eye. Lo and behold, it was our tickets for the next flight. They had fallen down to the bottom of the pouch. How did our tickets get into the tiny compartment? Without any remembrance of my careless act, evidently I'd put them there. Without those tickets our day would have gotten a whole lot more stressful. In fact that very morning we had witnessed a couple who had pleaded with the airline agent to let them on a flight despite the fact they had misplaced their tickets. The unwavering agent chided them, saying, "You need to go to the ticket counter in the main terminal and purchase new tickets."

With that scene fresh in my mind, I was horrified at what had almost happened. Steve was sitting quietly beside me working on a writing project. He was totally unaware of the situation. And here's the thing that haunts me. I almost said with stone-faced seriousness, "Steve, you had better be glad I found those tickets because if I hadn't, you would have gotten the blame for losing them." I was stunned and embarrassed that I would blame my totally innocent husband for something I had done.

When I finally admitted to Steve what a maniacal thought had passed through my head, he somehow saw the humor in it and we both laughed about it. But the sad questions I faced were: "Would I really have blamed him for losing the tickets? And if I had, would he have responded with justified ire...and a nasty conflict would have erupted?" I shudder to think what would have happened if I hadn't found the tickets and caught myself before I turned on Steve. The blame for any trouble that would have been caused would have rested squarely on my shoulders.

Yes, it's hard to catch ourselves before we subconsciously...or consciously...disrespect our husbands through our thoughts and actions. But how can we respond with gentleness and kindness when

that's not what we're receiving from our spouses? How do we forgive when we are hurt and treated unfairly? How can we respect our
husbands when we feel so unloved by them?

The Loneliest One

The loneliest one in this town tonight
Is not the one who's alone when they turn out the lights
It's the one who stares in the dark at the end of the day
Lying next to the one who feels so far away

The bed is warm, but the heart is cold
Not a word said, but the story is told
Where two people lie, and one of them cries
You'll find the loneliest one in this town tonight

Somebody once told me, these words are so true
Lonely is love if it's only you
And the saddest place on this earth is still
In arms that are empty that long to be filled[2]

If you are a wife who feels lonely like the lady in this lyric, or if
you feel mistreated, neglected, or unloved, then understandably you
want to know how you could ever show respect to your husband.
Let me offer a couple of ideas that might help you respond rightly
in the face of such disappointment.

The first thing to do when we are called to live out the love of
Christ in a difficult situation is to realize that ultimately our faith
and our hope is in God, not in our spouses. With that in mind, my
first suggestion is to…

Do What Is Right Because of Who Is Watching You

In 1 Peter 3:8-11 we are given some helpful instruction on how
to treat our spouses in a loving and respectful way. This instruction
applies even if our husbands are not believers.

To sum up, all of you be harmonious, sympathetic,

brotherly, kindhearted, and humble in spirit, not returning evil for evil or insult for insult, but giving a blessing instead; for you were called for the very purpose that you might inherit a blessing. For, the one who desires life, to love and see good days, must keep his tongue from evil and his lips from speaking deceit. He must turn away from evil and do good; he must seek peace and pursue it.

Why should we live our lives in respectful kindness toward our husbands when we aren't treated in a similar manner? The answer is found in the next verse: "The eyes of the Lord are toward the righteous, and his ears attend to their prayer, but the face of the Lord is against those who do evil" (verse 12).

The reason we should show respect and do what is right even when we are treated wrongly is because the eyes of God are watching us. Eventually each of us will stand in His presence and give an account for the deeds *we* have done. Your first responsibility is to God. You won't be held accountable to God for your mate's behavior, only your own.

My second suggestion is that you continue to pray earnestly that your husband's treatment of you will become the kind that fosters your respect and that you add a fast to your prayers. By willingly sacrificing something you need and/or enjoy, you can let God know how extremely serious you are about the health of your marriage.

Fasting is not one of my favorite activities. To go without the need and enjoyment of food is a tough task for me. However, I have seen the benefits of it, and know it yields some noticeable results, which spurs me on to let the old belly growl. The "empty tank reminder" in the midday is useful in cueing me to lift my prayers to the Lord. I have seen that benefit especially as Steve and I fasted as part of our prayers for our children. Not everyone can focus on food as something to sacrifice because of medical restrictions. In those cases, consider giving up something else that shows your heart's intention.

Fasting in a biblical way, according to Matthew 6, means that no one else knows it's being done. So don't inform your husband that you're fasting because of his behavior. Trust God.

Transformation can take place in a husband as a result of a wife's investment of prayer and fasting. Lindy's husband was literally one of the worst I have ever seen. Lindy committed to pray for her husband and fasted often. After two years of quietly and diligently taking him to the Lord with her sacrificial brand of prayers, an amazing change took place in her husband. It was truly a divine alteration! Her husband responded to the gospel message and gave his heart and life to Christ. From that point on he began to read and study the Scriptures and fellowship with other believers. He started to change. The great news for Lindy was that the changes in his personality reached into his life as a husband. The very sweet way he treats her today is nothing less than a miracle.

I can't guarantee that your husband will be as radically transformed as Lindy's husband, of course. God has given mankind free will, and He chooses not to override it. However, you can have confidence that when you pray and fast for your husband, God will hear your cries. He is pleased when His children bring their burdens to Him. As you cry out to Him, post this passage on the bulletin board of your heart: "Casting all your anxiety on Him, because He cares for you" (1 Peter 5:7).

For extra encouragement, remember this from James 5:13,16 from The Message: "Are you hurting? Pray....The prayer of a person living right with God is something powerful to be reckoned with."

Note: I encourage you wholeheartedly to pray for your husband and take your concerns to God. However, if you (or your kids) are being abused by your husband, seek help immediately.

A Hope and a Prayer for You

I realize that my husband, Steve, is an amazing, articulate man who willingly shares his heart. Although your husband may not be as open, my prayer is that you'll experience the wonderful kind of marriage we have.

One of the sweetest things Steve has ever said about me in a song lyric has become my chief goal as a wife. I hope you'll adopt this song as your wifely anthem.

You Make It Easy to Love

If I'm gonna make a livin,' I have to scratch and claw
Ain't no time for sittin,' no time at all
It's hard just getting by, it ain't never enough
But when it comes to you, babe
You make it easy to love

You make it easy to love
You make it seem downhill
I just want to put my feet up
That's how you make me feel
Sometimes I get weary
And the road gets rough
But what I like about you, babe
You make it easy to love

All I've ever seen is mountains on the way to my dreams
All my life I've been climbing, that's just the way it seems
But I'll keep pressin' on, even if it takes my blood
But I'm grateful for you, baby, 'cause there's one thing I'm sure of...

You make it easy to love
You make it seem downhill
I just want to put my feet up
That's how you make me feel
Sometimes I get weary
And the time gets tough
But what I love about you, baby
You make it easy to love[3]

10

I Want My Husband to Know

I Am Aware He Needs Me to Take Care of My Body

WHILE DRESSES, MAKEUP, JEWELRY, AND PERFUMES are important to a host of women, there is another aspect of personal appearance that is closely related to these interests yet is too often ignored, especially in the church. And it is an issue that can have a direct bearing on the quality of a marriage. That concern is the health of the body, specifically the physical condition of it. (One wife said, "I'm in shape. *Round* is a shape, isn't it?")

Think about the house you live in. Most of us take great pride in our homes. We keep the outside painted and in repair. We manicure the lawn, making sure it's neat and tidy. We plant flowers to add a little color to the landscape. We do all of these things to make sure our home has good "curb appeal." If we are careful to tend to the physical structure that we live in, doesn't it make sense that we should pay even more attention to what houses our soul and spirit? There should be great attention and effort exerted to make sure our "house" displays the proper "curve appeal," especially to our spouses.

I want my husband to know that physical health, fitness, and appearance are matters that are very important to me. And when it comes to us as a team, if *we* fail to take care of our bodies, we don't get to fully enjoy the other parts of our marriage. So I also want my husband to know that I need him to take care of his body too. We can't stop the aging process, but we can slow it down so we can enjoy to the max our life together.

I asked several hundred women to tell me what they and their husbands do to keep fit and healthy. It was shocking to see how many ladies either didn't respond at all or admitted that on the list of their priorities their concern for their health was further down than it should be. However, there were several who considered the issue as vital to the quality of their marriage, and from these women I gleaned the following helpful suggestions.

- Walk, ride bikes, skate, and swim
- We eat lots of whole grains, fruits, and vegetables
- We play golf
- We've joined a health club
- We keep regular doctor's appointments
- We sometimes walk together, which is wonderful prayer and talk time.
- Try to eat well and keep active. Neither of us smoke or drink
- We try to walk and though we do more trying than actually walking we refuse to give up
- I cook healthy, balanced meals
- We hike, camp, and do outside activities
- We try to watch our weight as a family
- I walk the dogs each night
- I garden and exercise at the church
- Use the treadmill during bad weather and walk outside when it's pretty
- Drink lots of water

- Take vitamins
- Get enough sleep
- My husband pushes me to exercise. I feel accountable to him
- I go to Curves and read literature on nutrition
- The only exercise I get is doing housework and chasing after small children. It might not be aerobic but I do expend a lot of energy

Sometimes women don't understand how important physical attractiveness is to some men. In her book *For Women Only*, Shaunti Feldhahn says it well:

> Because our husbands have pledged their faithfulness for better or for worse, and because we know "it's what's inside that counts," we can easily migrate to the idea that what's outside doesn't matter. But what's on the outside *does* matter. And when we seem to be willingly ignoring that truth, our men—even godly men who are devoted to us—end up feeling disregarded, disrespected, and hurt.[1]

With that observation in mind, I asked women to answer the question, "How important do you think your physical appearance is to your husband?" Their responses were very interesting. Some of the women minimized the importance of their outward appearance while others seemed to understand that men are very visual people. Look at some of the comments from the women.

- He never criticizes my looks, and he appreciates the fact that I'm always dieting.
- Finally the waist rolls don't matter as much as they once did. I think my husband accepts me even though I don't look the way I once did.

- He always tells me he loves me and I'm beautiful.

- I think physical appearance is very important in a relationship. My husband compliments me on how I look.

- He never criticizes my appearance, but he rarely compliments me. I know he does appreciate it when I make an effort to look extra nice, even if he may not say so. I do know he responds differently to me now as a heavier person than he did when I was thinner.

- It means a lot. He doesn't criticize me about it, but I know he's concerned about my health because he keeps bugging me about exercising.

- I need my husband to give me more positive feedback.

- He always acknowledges when I wear something new or special. It makes me feel good about myself.

- My husband says, "Honey, you're not fat, you're fluffy."

- My husband cared a lot about physical appearance. Maybe that's why he had an affair with a younger and prettier woman. We're not married anymore.

- My appearance is very important to him and sometimes it causes arguments. He criticizes my weight and acne at least twice a month because it is that important to him.

- My appearance isn't terribly important, but he compliments me often on my weight loss and appreciates my new appearance and new energy.

- It's not only important to my husband, but my personal appearance is important to me. I want to look and feel the best I can so I can be all I can be for the Lord and represent Him.

- His eyes say more than all the words.

- He likes my appearance. He says he likes everything

about me even stretch marks on my legs. He gets upset when I criticize myself.

- He thinks I could work on my weight and that I don't have a very pretty face. He says he has a hard time being attracted to me.

- He likes me to look good, but usually doesn't comment.

- It's important to my husband that I not be obese. But a few extra pounds does not seem to bother him. He tells me I'm pretty.

- My husband likes me to be dressed appropriately for occasions. He rarely comments about appearance positively or negatively.

- It is important that I take care of myself. He tells me he likes the way I look. I'm very heavy now, but when we got married I was a nice, slender size. Even though I know he wishes I would lose weight, he never criticizes me.

With so many women revealing how important they think their appearance is to their husbands, I thought it would be interesting to see what men have to say about how important the physical appearance of their wives is to them. The following comments were their husband's responses to the question, "How important is your wife's physical appearance to you?

- It's important to me, but I will take my wife however she wants to be.

- It is important because she definitely feels better and is in a better mental place when she is focused on staying fit.

- I don't like it when my wife is too fat or too thin.

- Her appearance is important to me. We are both growing older and appearances change. Her warm heart is the best part of her.

- My wife's physical appearance is very important to me. I am influenced by the visual appeal.

- My wife has let her appearance go in the last few years. Satan uses her physical appearance to lead my thoughts away from her real beauty. I like to look at beautiful things.

- Her appearance is a good indication of her health. I want her to be around for a long time for me to love.

- It is nice if she is attractive to me, but the way she treats me and her personality are more important.

- My wife is my sunshine and my best friend, and I love her even in the morning before she puts her face on.

- When she take care of her appearance it makes it easier to show her physical affection.

- Her appearance is important to me. I'm afraid she'll become overweight like her mother.

- When she is happy about her appearance she is willing to be more sexually active in our marriage.

- When my wife looks good, it makes it easier to commit to her and be faithful to her.

- Physical appearance is important to the attraction that bonds a man and woman.

- I feel proud to be seen with my wife when she looks attractive.

- When my wife feels self-confident in her appearance it helps her inner beauty come out.

- When my wife looks good, it reflects on me. I feel proud when my wife is attractive.

- It affects her attitude when she's healthy and fit. She is more upbeat and happy.

- Our marriage is better the better she looks because she feels more positive about herself.

- When my wife is unhappy with her appearance, she doesn't want to go out and do anything. When she's happy, then I'm happy.

Now, one more list of male responses that I think most of us ladies will find very interesting. These came from several men at a retreat where Steve spoke. I sent a stack of survey forms with him that contained a question that I wasn't sure the men would answer. Much to my surprise, about 75 percent of them did respond and quite candidly. When you see what the question asks as well as realize that they could answer it without consequence, then you'll understand why so many eagerly responded. I don't have room for all of their statements but there is plenty of them to prove the point that men do indeed consider their wives' appearance as a very important aspect of their relationship.

The question that was asked was, "What would you say to your wife about her appearance if you were certain you wouldn't get in trouble for it?"

- I love it when you do your hair and makeup and wish you'd do it more often.

- You're getting your mother's figure.

- I wish you would exercise more.

- I'm worried about you. I don't want you to die young like your dad.

- I wish you wouldn't complain about your eating and weight unless you're going to do something about it. I get tired of hearing you put yourself down, but then you don't change the things you're doing that keep you that way.

- I wish you would lose the excess weight you've gained since we got married.

- I know you've wanted braces for a long time. But being the kind of mother you are, you always put the kids first. Well, the kids are on their own now, and it's time you did something for yourself. Go ahead and get the braces.

- You know that you're all I've ever wanted in a woman. But please dress and make yourself up on a regular basis.

- I need you to do something about your morning breath.

I can only guess at what motivated these men to keep quiet about the feelings they wrote down on paper. They probably feared reactions such as intense anger, looks of hurt, tears, cold shoulders, and other cold body parts, and even flying frying pans. Who knows?

As Steve and I pored over the "secret, unsaid longings" about wives' appearance, Steve said a couple of things I thought were very astute. First he observed, "I feel sorry for the guys who wrote these responses who have wives whose struggle to lose, or even in some cases, to gain weight, are hormonal or hereditary related. There's no way they should speak their hearts." Then he said, "But I also wonder how many of these guys not only keep their 'dangerous' thoughts to themselves but also keep their encouraging, helpful comments silent."

Steve followed that comment with the suggestion that some husbands may fear that their compliments about the positive things their wives do will cause them to think they've done enough and then stop doing things like dieting and exercise. He added, "I have a feeling that if these guys looked for positive things to say to their wives, no matter how insignificant they may seem, they'd help their wives keep motivated, and both of them would see more results. I definitely wouldn't recommend they express the negatives, but they should always look for opportunities to say the positives."

Recently, a friend shared a letter that is a good example of a spouse recognizing the good things the other is doing. In this case, the wife did the writing to her husband. They have, as a couple and also as an entire family, chosen a change of lifestyle. While weight issues have plagued them their whole married life, they have found a new source of strength by taking on this "stronghold" together. And, together, they are experiencing success. She tenderly wrote:

> To My Precious Husband
>
> Praise the Lord! I am so thankful that you followed through with my request and gave me ten weeks at Weight Watchers for my birthday. And not only that, you allowed me to give you those same ten weeks for your birthday coming up soon. I've been so proud of your discipline and initial weight loss of 13.5 pounds in one week. WOW! I'm proud that you've chosen to become accountable with a friend and that you work out three times a week. I know we've tried this for sixteen years unsuccessfully, gaining back what we've lost. But I'm praying that this time will be different. I've gained a sense of control in the kitchen and pantry that I've prayed for, and I'm enjoying cooking again. It's because I have a plan...I have some direction. I hope and pray that I am a contributor to your success. I want to help you to be healthy and fit. I count it a privilege to be your helpmeet in this way. I want to grow old and healthy with you. I believe, with God's help, I will.

Three Steps Toward a Better Us

There are at least three areas where a couple can "team together" and encourage each other in achieving and maintaining better health and fitness. Together they can help attend to their "curve appeal." Keep in mind that even though we can be a cheerleader for one another, ultimately the work has to be done on an individual level as suggested in a passage found in 2 Corinthians 7:1: "Therefore, having these promises, beloved, *let us cleanse ourselves* from all defilement of flesh and spirit, perfecting holiness in the fear of God."

When I did a close study of what this passage means I was struck by something I had not seen before. We are to cleanse ourselves. The passage doesn't say, "Wait and let God cleanse you from all defilement." No, the Lord expects us to participate in our "spiritual hygiene" with Him by going often to Him for redemptive cleansing from defilements such as greed, anxiety, and lust.

This "cleanse ourselves" process is true for our spiritual lives, but it is also true for our physical beings. To illustrate, notice how most of us can go to bed with freshly brushed teeth but wake up with breath that could derail a freight train. Did we get up in the night and eat? No. Morning death…er breath…is simply a part of the daily decay of the human condition. But in order to reestablish the oral freshness what do we do? We brush our teeth again. If we're able-bodied, no one else does the brushing for us. We cleanse ourselves.

Too many of us who have been taught that spiritually we can do nothing for ourselves make the mistake of letting this attitude spill over into the physical realm. Consequently, we don't do what we ought to do. For instance, I remember as an overweight teenager praying in the night, "Lord, You said that if I ask You for anything in faith and believe You will hear and answer my prayer, that You will grant my petition. My request is that when I wake up in the morning I want to not be overweight. I want You to make me thin. I pray in Jesus' name. Amen."

Can you guess what happened while I slept? You're right! Absolutely nothing. It's not that God couldn't miraculously remove the pounds, the reason He didn't was so I could understand that I had to be involved in the needed change by exercising some fork control. If He had done it without my involvement, He would have to have done it every morning for me because I would have continued to overeat.

Not only is it not God's responsibility to cleanse us physically, it is also not our spouses' job to cleanse us. Neither mate is responsible to track the other's dietary intake or to dish out portions of food on each other's plates, unless, of course, they agree to it. But ultimately, we are to take care of the physical cleansing and conditioning of our own individual bodies.

I want my husband to know that with our courage firmly in place to be personally responsible for our physical condition, we can do the following things together.

Step 1: Cultivate Good Eating Habits

One of the best quips about eating that I have ever heard is one that became my personal goal. "Don't live to eat, eat to live." I heard this many years ago at about the time a very popular restaurant chain opened their doors here in the Nashville area. Their feature foods were fried chicken, huge biscuits, French fries, and the sweetest tea on the planet. Our family frequented the place because we could get the "all you can eat" deal and feed a family of four cheaply. However, if we had a dollar for every fat gram we consumed during our visits to their greasy tables we'd have enough money to buy an island!

When we finally noticed our waistlines were starting to look like ( ) instead of) (, we changed our dietary ways. The first thing we did was cease our journeys to that particular restaurant. Instead, I started cooking at home using healthy oils, whole grains, low-fat milk, and other ingredients that contributed to our weight loss.

I'm happy to report that for more than 20 years the habits we developed then are still in place, and they continue to pay off. We're not only lighter, but we also don't get sick as often as we used to.

As I thought through our current, regular eating habits, the following little things have translated into big results for us:

- Homemade "health cookies" made with real oats, raisins, nuts, honey, and whole grains
- Buying half-size cans of soda and drinking them only occasionally
- Taking the skin off the chicken
- Buying 1%-fat milk

- Being careful of what we bring into the house (baked chips instead of fried, for example)
- Fasting together as a couple at least once a week for a minimum of 18 hours
- Having a vegetarian supper once a week or, better yet, having meat only once a week

If you don't have a weight problem but your husband does, make concessions for his struggle. For instance, don't insist on having Rocky Road ice cream in the house if this is a temptation for him. Get your "fix" while you're out.

I don't suggest you initiate the request, but if your spouse wants to join a health club or go on a diet program, encourage him to do it. And don't complain about the money. It will be a great investment. Besides, more than likely he is not doing this just for himself, but for you as well. Be supportive and helpful, but ultimately he's the one who has to *want* to do it.

Step 2: Commit to Exercise

At my request Steve bought a treadmill for me for Valentine's Day a few years ago. (Every husband, by the way, should be aware that a treadmill, like a health club or diet club membership, is a gift a wife has to ask for. To give it to her without her requesting it is a dangerous act on a man's part, unless of course, he's an avid fan of marital conflict. If your husband doesn't know this, gently clue him in.)

I love the treadmill, and Steve hates it. He doesn't like the idea of walking for 45 minutes and not going anywhere. So I am the lone user of the walking machine that, to Steve's surprise and delight, is used almost every day. If the weather is nice I might walk outside, but most of time I'm pounding the sweat conveyer in our upstairs room (that's where the TV is).

While I walk for the vascular benefits, I also admit that every step is taken with consideration of how the walking will contribute to how I look for Steve. He returns the favor by pounding the asphalt with amazing regularity. His regimen, since knee surgery in 1990 that was caused by running long distances excessively, is a four-mile brisk walk every other day. He allows his knees to heal for a day before making demands of them again. I appreciate his wise approach in regard to conserving his joints. I also appreciate his willingness to keep his heart and muscles strong and active by putting in the miles.

Step 3: Checkups with Your Doctor

Steve is a fair-skinned man and is prone to dermatological issues. For that reason he has been faithful to have his skin checked regularly and at the first sign of any potential problems. With enough scary episodes in the past, as well as one unforgettable, prescribed use of some really nasty "chemo cream" that he had to apply for 30 days on a precancerous spot, he feels motivated to keep a constant eye on his epidermis. One reason I am grateful that Steve tends to his skin is that it tells me that he cares enough about us that he wants to hang around as long as possible.

My act of reciprocation in terms of regularly going to the doctor is to go to a gynecologist. I'm not a fan of the visit and would likely never venture to his office if it weren't so important. For that reason, when I go I tell Steve, "I'm doing this for you, you know." The truth is, that is indeed the main reason I endure such an invasive exam.

Going to the doctor for preventative screenings, scannings, and normal selective exams is a wise thing to do. It costs money, time, and dignity. Disrobing, probing, poking, sticking, and feeling around on our person in the coldness of a doctor's office is not fun. Yet the price for squeezing as many good together years out of life is one that is worth the return.

With that last thought in mind I close with the familiar sentiment, "Sometimes we don't appreciate what we have until it's taken away." How true. I can think of no one in our lives who made that point more clear than a widow lady we lived next to for a number of years. Her name was Mary Williams.

One night we invited Mary to come to our house for dinner. While talking with her about her family we asked her to tell us the one thing she missed the most about the absence of her deceased beloved husband, John. What she said impacted us greatly. At the time we were married just a few years with two very small children. Though we talked about the wisdom we received from Mary that night from time to time through the following decades, it wasn't until many years later that Steve put down in lyric form the wisdom in what Mary shared with us. I hope her words will impact you the way they did us.

What If

Mary said, "There's a lot of things I've missed about John.
In these fifteen years since he's been gone.
Lord knows it's a mighty long list, if I had to choose just one.
He used to ask a question, and sometimes I hear it when I'm all alone"

He'd say, "What if we go out to dinner tonight?
What if we take a walk in the full moonlight?
What if we go take in a movie, just me and my best friend?"
Oh, how I wish I could "what if"
With John
One more time again.

She said, "It's funny how a question can hold so many answers
More than I'd ever need
I never had to wonder, I never had to ask,
Did he care about me?
I feel sad for the women who've never known a man
Who understood like mine.
Love is a diamond, and if you're going to have it
You gotta spend some time."

He'd say, "What if we go out to dinner tonight?
What if we take a walk in the full moonlight?
What if we take a ride on the Harley, just you and me in the wind?

Or what if we go look at antiques, just want to be with my best friend?"
Oh, how I wish I could what if
With John
One more time again[2]

So I encourage you to take care of yourself physically. Also gently help your spouse if he needs support in this area. The goal is to please each other and make your marriage happy and exciting as long as possible.

How Best to Love
Your Husband

YOU MAY RECALL IN CHAPTER 4 I suggested that only 7 percent of communication is verbal and 93 percent is nonverbal. Though the verbal may represent a relatively small percentage, it is still very important! As you close this book and ponder the practical ideas of what to say to your beloved, may God give you a spirit of graciousness and love in *how* you convey your heart to your husband.

Body language and tone of voice speak volumes. With that in mind, please don't forget that sometimes our actions can drown out the actual words we use, no matter how eloquent or articulate they may be. I have known some wives who, while attempting to alter their men's behavior or to get their way in a matter, have made some grave, nonverbal mistakes. Pouting like a child, pointing out his mistakes like an unreasonable teacher, and even using sex to manipulate them will rarely, if ever, accomplish the goal of effective communication. I urge you to avoid these kinds of dangerous tactics.

Instead, consider this verse from Psalm 4 that can help you communicate the right words in the right way:

> Many are saying, "Who will show us any good?" Lift
> up the light of Your countenance upon us, O LORD!
> (verse 6).

What an incredible opportunity this passage presents to you as a wife. Perhaps the best way you can show your husband how much you love him is to do everything possible to allow God to shine through you.

It is my prayer that in all you say and in how you say it your husband will see the light of the comforting countenance of our heavenly Father. As you strive to represent Him in your marriage, He will shine brightly and inspire you and your husband as you grow closer together.

Notes

Chapter 1

1. Anne Williamson, "Never Say Never," Times & Seasons Music, 1974. Not recorded.
2. Rick Renner, *Sparkling Gems from the Greek* (Tulsa, OK: Teach All Nations, 2003), p. 524.
3. Ibid.
4. Ibid., pp. 524-25.
5. Ibid., p. 525.
6. Steve Chapman, "Feels Like Love," Times & Seasons Music/BMI, 2002. Album: The Miles, #SACD-2803.
7. Steve Chapman, "That Way Again," Times & Seasons Music/BMI, 2005. Album: That Way Again, #SACD-126.

Chapter 3

1. Steve Chapman, "We Will Love This Child," Times & Seasons Music/BMI. Album: That Way Again, #SACD-126.
2. Neil Anderson, *Finding Freedom in a Sex-Obsessed World* (Eugene, OR: Harvest House Publishers, 2004), p. 114.
3. Steve Chapman, "We Get in Trouble When We Kiss," Times & Seasons Music, 2005. Not recorded.

Chapter 4

1. Nathan Chapman, "Weather It All," Times & Seasons Music/BMI, 2001. Album: The Miles, #SACD-2803.
2. Steve Chapman, "Reachable," Times & Seasons Music/BMI. Album: Family Favorites, #SACD-105.
3. Steve Chapman, "Easy to Steal," Times & Seasons Music/BMI, 2006. Not available on an album yet. Administered by Gaither Copyright Management.
4. Steve Chapman, "Faithful to You," Times & Seasons Music, 1992. Album: Kiss of Hearts, #SACD-8000.

Chapter 5

1. Shaunti Feldhahn, *For Women Only* (Sisters, OR: Multnomah, 2004).
2. James Montgomery Boice, *The Parables of Jesus* (Chicago: Moody Press, 1983), p. 104.
3. Steve Chapman, "Play or Not," Times & Seasons Music/BMI, 2005. Not recorded.

Chapter 6

1. Quoted in Annie Chapman, *The Mother-in-Law Dance* (Eugene, OR: Harvest House Publishers, 2004), p. 84.
2. Steve Chapman, "Mystery of the Season," Times & Seasons Music/BMI. Album: Coming Home for Christmas.
3. Annie Chapman, *Mother-in-Law Dance,* pp. 57-59.
4. Steve Chapman, "Man in Aisle Number Two," Times & Seasons Music. Album: Silver Bridge, #SACD-97.

Chapter 7

1. Steve Chapman, "Bother My Baby," Times & Seasons Music/BMI. Album: Steppin' in the Tracks, #SACD-1200.

Chapter 8

1. Steve Chapman, "Wednesday's Prayer," Times & Seasons Music/BMI, 1999. Album: At the Potter's House, #SACD-110.
2. Steve Chapman, "Love Was Spoken," Times & Seasons Music/BMI, 1991. Album: Love Was Spoken, #SACD-1020.
3. Steve Chapman, "Daddy's Shoes," Times & Seasons Music/BMI. Album: Steppin' in the Tracks, #SACD-1200.
4. Steve Chapman, "Don't Unpack Your Bags," Times & Seasons Music/BMI. Album: That Way Again, #SACD-126.
5. Steve Chapman, "Before There Was You," Times & Seasons Music/BMI. Album: Tools for the Trade, #SACD-7000.
6. Steve Chapman, "One Man Prayed," Times & Seasons Music/BMI. Album: Steppin' in the Tracks, #SACD-1200.

Chapter 9

1. Shaunti Feldhahn, *For Women Only* (Sisters, OR: Multnomah Publishers, 2004), pp. 67-68.
2. Steve Chapman, "The Loneliest One," Times & Seasons Music/BMI. Not recorded.
3. Steve Chapman, "You Make It Easy to Love," Times & Seasons Music/BMI, 2006. Not recorded.

Chapter 10

1. Shaunti Feldhahn, *For Women Only* (Sisters, OR: Multnomah Publishers, 2004), pp. 163-64.
2. Steve Chapman, "What If," Times & Seasons Music/BMI, 2005. Album: That Way Again, #SACD-126.

To contact Annie Chapman or find out more about the Chapmans' speaking and recording ministry, write to:

Steve and Annie Chapman
S&A Family, Inc.
PO Box 337
Pleasant View, TN 37146

or visit their website:

www.steveandanniechapman.com

HARVEST HOUSE
PUBLISHERS

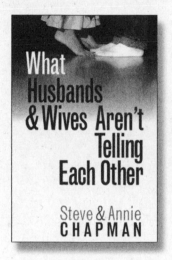

WHAT HUSBANDS AND WIVES AREN'T TELLING EACH OTHER
Steve and Annie Chapman

What is the greatest challenge of your marriage? What is your greatest concern regarding financial health? What do you and your spouse do for fun? Exploring these and other questions, Steve and Annie Chapman draw on their more than 30 years of married life, God's Word, and a survey of almost 500 couples to explore foundational conversations that highlight the truths upon which successful marriages are built. As you examine real-life situations, you'll discover the keys to making marriage more satisfying:

- finding spiritual wholeness

- creating a partnership in love, cooperation, and mutual submission

- realizing the importance of flexibility

- recapturing the laughter lost in daily living

- developing a mature love that will last a lifetime

As you explore vital topics seldom discussed, your marriage will become deeper and more fulfilling.

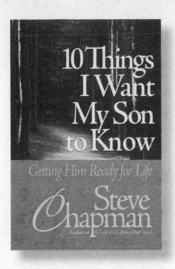

10 THINGS I WANT MY SON TO KNOW
Steve Chapman

Fatherhood. What an amazing gift from God! Being a dad requires love, humor, wisdom...and nerves of steel. And that's only the beginning. Turning to the only "manual" that comes with children, Steve Chapman shares his top-10 principles drawn from the Bible's wisdom and practical experience that helped him raise a son dedicated to the Lord. Whether you're just starting out on the "papa" road or have traveled part of the distance, you'll appreciate the practical information, hands-on suggestions, and often humorous examples Steve shares to help you raise a son who will be a man of God and a man of honor.

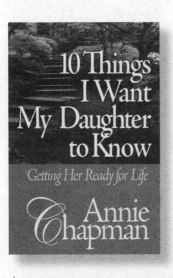

10 THINGS I WANT MY DAUGHTER TO KNOW
Annie Chapman

What a blessing God has given you...a beautiful daughter! As you gaze into her future, what values and life skills would you like her to have? What activities can you do together to help her become a woman of God? Drawing on her experiences, the wisdom of God's Word, and insights from other mothers, Annie Chapman highlights 10 essential truths and how to share them with your daughter. You'll also discover guidance for developing faith, discernment, trust, and integrity from the lives of women in the Bible. Speaking from her heart, Annie candidly reveals the ups and downs of motherhood to help you navigate the sometimes tricky yet always fulfilling role of "Mom."

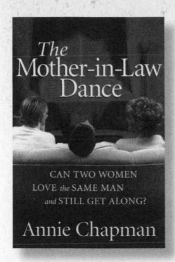

THE MOTHER-IN-LAW DANCE
Annie Chapman

Describing the often delicate relationship between mother-in-law and daughter-in-law as a dance, Annie Chapman candidly discusses the twists and turns of this important connection and provides practical advice to help you better relate with your mother- or daughter-in-law. Drawing on years of experience, real-life input from other women, and biblical insights, she reveals simple steps to successfully building a great relationship, dealing with new traditions and activities, overcoming hurts and conflicts, setting realistic boundaries, and much more.

As you establish a rhythm of love and grace, you'll find that you and your in-law can become friends—even close friends!

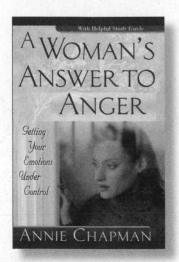

A WOMAN'S ANSWER TO ANGER
Annie Chapman

Do you struggle to control an explosive temper, wish you could take back angry words, or don't understand why you get so upset all the time? Annie's story of her own struggle with anger will help you find solace, comfort, and hope. As you journey with her toward peace, you'll discover biblical principles and practical advice that will help you conquer intense emotions, negative words, and angry actions, including how to gain control of what you say, do, and think, fix problems created by angry reactions, and deal with irritating people who treat you poorly

With compassion and understanding, Annie shows that it is possible to put anger in its place and get on with the joy of living.